THE
GREAT
WESTERN
SOCIETY

THE
GREAT WESTERN SOCIETY

A TALE OF ENDEAVOUR & SUCCESS

ANTHONY BURTON

PEN & SWORD
TRANSPORT

AN IMPRINT OF PEN & SWORD BOOKS LTD.
YORKSHIRE – PHILADELPHIA

First published in Great Britain in 2019 by
PEN & SWORD TRANSPORT
An imprint of
Pen & Sword Books Ltd
Yorkshire - Philadelphia

ISBN 978 1 52671 945 4

Typeset in 10.5/13.5 pt Palatino
Typeset by Aura Technology and Software Services, India
Printed and bound in India by Replika Press Pvt. Ltd.

Pen & Sword Books Ltd incorporates the Imprints of Pen & Sword Books Archaeology, Atlas, Aviation, Battleground, Discovery, Family History, History, Maritime, Military, Naval, Politics, Railways, Select, Transport, True Crime, Fiction, Frontline Books, Leo Cooper, Praetorian Press, Seaforth Publishing, Wharncliffe and White Owl.

For a complete list of Pen & Sword titles please contact

PEN & SWORD BOOKS LIMITED
47 Church Street, Barnsley, South Yorkshire, S70 2AS, England
E-mail: enquiries@pen-and-sword.co.uk
Website: www.pen-and-sword.co.uk

Or
PEN AND SWORD BOOKS
1950 Lawrence Rd, Havertown, PA 19083, USA
E-mail: Uspen-and-sword@casematepublishers.com
Website: www.penandswordbooks.com

Contents

Preface

I have known Didcot Rail Centre for many years. I had visited it for pleasure many times and had even filmed there when making a BBC documentary to celebrate GWR 150. And as I lived in Oxfordshire for many years and frequently had to take the train to London, I always looked out of the window as we drew into Didcot station in the hope of seeing something on the move or an interesting item parked outside the shed. So I was delighted to be invited to write this history of the Great Western Society. But, like I suspect many visitors who come to the Centre, I had only a hazy idea about the work that had gone in to creating the experience I was enjoying. Visiting it again with the book in mind was a very different experience; exciting certainly, but the overwhelming impression was one of admiration for what has been done and is still being achieved.

Research was based in part on documentary sources – I was supplied with Newsletters from the earliest days and copies of the *Great Western Echo*. These were invaluable but I could never have written the book without the help of the volunteers and members of the permanent staff who took the time to show me round and to sit and talk about their own particular areas of interest. I also received help from members of the Firefly Trust and the Swindon Panel Society. There are too many for me to name every individual, but I owe a special debt to Richard Croucher for organising the various visits that I made to Didcot in 2017 and 2018. I am also grateful to everyone who supplied the photos that illustrate this book – the vast majority have been supplied by Frank Dumbleton and Laurence Waters. The book could not have been produced without them. Various people have read the text and offered their comments, but any errors that remain are entirely mine.

We live in an age of metric measurements, but in the days when the Great Western were building railways, locomotives and rolling stock, everything was in the older imperial measurements. I have used those measurements here, because they seem more appropriate. A locomotive might run at Didcot at a working pressure of 200 pounds per square inch, and that is what the pressure gauge will indicate – not 13.8 bar. Similarly, when the engineer decreed that an engine should have 6ft drive wheels that is what he got, not 1.83 metres.

Anthony Burton
Stroud 2019

CHAPTER ONE

Why Great Western?

It perhaps seems slightly perverse to start an account of the Great Western Society by appearing to question its very existence. But it is a question worth asking because it seems there is no railway company anywhere in the world that has attracted so many supporters nor roused such enthusiasm. So, what is the answer? In fact, there is no single answer, but instead a happy combination of factors that combine to make the company's title more than a mere example of public relations hyperbole; the Western Railway was, indeed, Great.

The first factor has to be the man who became the Chief Engineer responsible for planning and building the line, Isambard Kingdom Brunel. His name regularly crops up in any list of greatest Britons of all time and almost invariably he would be the only engineer to get a mention. He is an instantly recognisable figure with his stove pipe hat and big cigar but what makes him stand out from his contemporaries is the breadth of his achievements, his audacity and his absolute determination to do things his own way regardless of what the rest of the world might think. All these traits appear when we look at the Great Western.

It is still astonishing to realise that when he was appointed as Chief Engineer, Brunel was still only 27 years old, and yet was quite happy, from the first, to ignore precedents and the notions of more experienced engineers. When George Stephenson first began building steam locomotives, he did so for existing colliery lines that had originally been worked by horses. When he moved on to the more important lines, the Stockton & Darlington and the first inter-city route, the Liverpool & Manchester, he simply stuck with the same gauge, which would eventually become standardised as 4ft 8½in. Brunel began from a very different position, by asking a very fundamental question; what would be the best gauge to ensure fast, comfortable travel? And, of course, the answer he came up with was his broad gauge of 7ft. The way he laid out his track was also fundamentally different, as we shall see later. He was a man who made his own decisions. When a gentleman by the name of Dr Dionysus Lardner, considered one of the most eminent

scientists of the day, declared that travellers would not survive a
journey through the proposed tunnel at Box, he ignored him and
was proved right. When other engineers declared that the flat brick
arches of the bridge across the Thames at Maidenhead couldn't
possibly stand, he built it anyway – and it still survives to this day.
Not that he got everything right. If his own ideas about locomotive
construction had been allowed to prevail, the result would have
been a very poor service indeed. Fortunately, he had enough sense
to hire a brilliant young man called Daniel Gooch, who at once
put the Great Western at the forefront of development. Brunel's
determination to go for the new and experimental did not always
lead to triumph – and few of his decisions were more disastrous
than that to install the atmospheric railway when extending the
route westward from Exeter. Its failure might have resulted in many
companies giving their engineer the boot; but such was Brunel's
reputation and charisma that he was simply allowed to replace the
system with a conventional railway and to continue his work of
extending the Great Western Railway empire.

The Great Western continued to spread, from London westward to the tip of Cornwall, up into South Wales and north towards the Midlands. It covered such an extensive area that when other railways were grouped together into four main line companies in 1923, the GWR was the only one to retain its identity. This is another factor that ensured its popularity, its sheer longevity. Even after nationalisation, when it finally lost its noble title and became merely mundane Western Region, the area covered had scarcely changed and the character of the GWR lived on, particularly in its fine fleet of locomotives. No other main line railway company had such a long life. And for much of that time, it retained its innovative spirit that had begun during the reign of its first engineer, thanks to the Great Western's ability to attract mechanical engineers of immense skill and imagination, such as George Jackson Churchward and Charles Benjamin Collett. The company was also leading the way in such important elements as the introduction of the electric

The Great Western was always looking for new ways to attract passengers, so the Cornish coast became the more exotic Cornish Riviera.

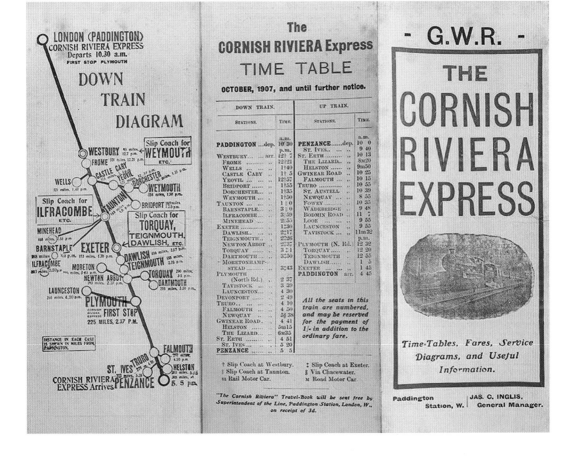

telegraph and being recorded as the first railway in the world to have a locomotive travelling at over 100 miles per hour, with *City of Truro* in 1904, even if some railway historians have questioned whether it actually happened. There was always something new for railway enthusiasts to admire on the Great Western.

There is another factor here that is not perhaps so immediately obvious; the GWR were superb publicists, who presented an enticing image of what the company had to offer. From the start, they encouraged commercial companies to produce guides to the line and were probably the first railway company to employ an

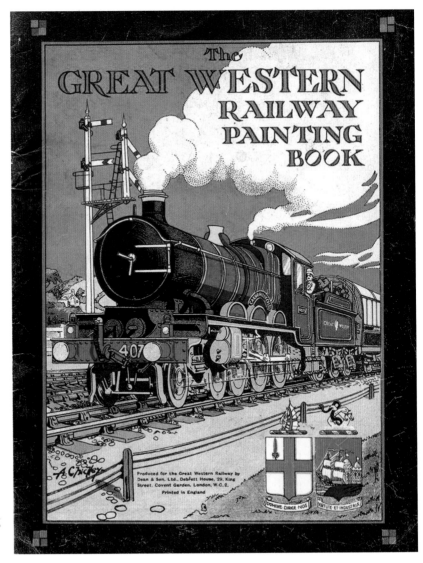

Many items were produced to attract the young – who would be the paying passengers of the future.

advertising agency. But the advertising really got into its stride in the twentieth century, and especially in the 1920s. The company realised it had a unique status, and while the new groupings were just starting to create an identity for themselves, the GWR stressed tradition. The coaching stock reverted to the old chocolate-and-cream livery, yet at the same time they promoted the exciting image of express locomotives, handsome in green with brass topped chimneys and sloping boilers. They were telling a story; we have been around a long time and have a great tradition, but we have not stood still – we will carry you to your destination in comfortable coaches hauled by the very latest, most powerful and fastest locomotives.

The main objective was to encourage passengers to travel, especially to the holiday destinations of the West Country. Special trains were given such exotic names as *The Cornish Riviera Express,* suggesting that a holiday in Newquay would be much the same as one in Nice or Cannes. Magnificent posters were produced, together with a series of guides called *Holiday Haunts,* and the young were tempted with jigsaws and painting books. All this was aimed at the general public to encourage ticket sales, but there was a growing realisation among the newly formed publicity department that there was also a lot of interest in the locomotives for their own sake. 1911 saw the publication of *Names of Engines* that would be expanded over the years into several editions of *GWR Engines, Names, Numbers, Types & Classes.* A new hobby had been born, train spotting, that was to grow in popularity through the years, encouraged by other publications, written as was the guide to GWR engines, by W.G.C. Chapman, aimed at 'Boys of All Ages' – girls it seems were not even considered as possible railway enthusiasts at that time. They were hugely successful – *The 10.30 Limited,* for example, sold over 70,000 copies in six months, figures which, alas, the modern railway historian can only dream of.

The publicity machine helped to create a huge interest in railways, but very especially in the Great Western. The line attracted a loyal following of enthusiasts who would look down at lesser breeds of railway and many of them retained their childhood enthusiasm for the rest of their lives. It was these young enthusiasts who were to start a process that would ensure that the legacy of the Great Western Railway would live on.

CHAPTER TWO

Beginnings

In 2017, a dismantled footbridge arrived at the Didcot Rail Centre from Southall. Outwardly it was nothing very special, the sort of utilitarian structure you can find at stations all over Britain. But it has a special place in the history of the Great Western Society. It was here that four schoolboy trainspotters used to meet regularly: Jon Barlow; Angus Davis; Mike Peat; and Graham Perry. In April 1961, Angus had just seen his copy of *The Railway Magazine.* They all knew that British Rail was planning to end the age of steam, in favour of diesel and electric and now the list of steam locomotives that they intended to preserve from that era had been published. Out of the 73 classes to be saved, only 10 were from the Great Western, and Angus discovered to his horror that notable absences from the GWR list were Halls, Manors and 14xx. He dashed off to meet his friends on the footbridge and they decided something had to be done; in particular they wanted to save an example of the 14xxs.

Many enthusiasts might have gone for a Manor or a Hall, but they were more interested in the less obviously exotic 14xx. This was a class of locomotives that took you right back to the age of Victoria, for they were based with a few modifications on the 517 class, designed for branch line passenger trains by George Armstrong, that first went into production in 1868. They were redesigned by Charles Collett in 1932, with a few refinements including the addition of windows front and back to the cab, which must have been good news for the drivers. They were still 0-4-2 tank engines and kept the tall chimney and high dome that characterised so many nineteenth century engines. One can understand why they were worthy of preservation, because they have a number of points of interest. In spite of their general, rather old-fashioned appearance, these were noted for being able to move pretty quickly when given the chance. There is a story that on one occasion, running with just a parcels coach, it actually beat the famous *Bristolian* into Paddington.

The class was in fact more up to date than first appearance suggests. Saddle tanks are comparatively easy to manufacture;

Where it all began; Graham Perry posing on the footbridge at Southall.

make the saddle separately and fit it over the boiler. But this class introduced what was then the fairly new Belpaire boiler with a flat top so that the saddle no longer could be easily fitted, hence the pannier tanks at the sides of the boiler. The 14xxs were also adapted for use with autocoach of which more later. So, for enthusiasts there was a lot of interest in these particular engines. They were certainly interesting enough for the boys to decide they should do something about it. They all went off to Angus's house where over cheese on toast they discussed what should be done. The upshot was that they decided to form the 14xx Preservation Society, and as Jon was the only one with a typewriter he was given the job of writing to *The Railway Magazine* to propose the idea of saving a 14xx. The letter gave no hint of the age of the sender, simply signed J.L. Barlow. It began:

> 'I am thinking of launching a campaign to purchase a "14xx" (former 48XX) class 0-4-2 locomotive from British Railways, with the purpose of preserving it in running order. The cost is £1,150 plus extra costs, such as having "48XX" number-plates cast and repainting in Great Western livery. If sufficient interest is obtained, perhaps a pull-and-push coach also might be preserved.'

The boys waited for the letter to appear – nothing in the next issue, nor the next. Summer holidays came round and they went their separate ways, Jon for an adventure holiday in the Lake District, others for a rail trip round Scottish engine sheds. But then the letter finally appeared, and because Jon's address had been used, he started getting replies. By then they were all back at home, and Frank Dumbleton, another schoolboy spotter, was on the famous bridge when Jon arrived with the news. Frank remembered him arriving on his bike, rumbling over the wooden floorboards and cycling straight past the notice warning of dire penalties for anyone using a bicycle on the bridge. He was waving a sheath of letters, one of which from a Mr. B.H. Farmer of Cambridge enclosed £10. It seemed the preservation society was about to become a reality.

It was decided to form a committee and as not all the gang was available for an instant meeting, Frank Dumbleton was recruited. He was later removed on the grounds that, being at boarding school, he wouldn't be available for meetings. This turned out to be a temporary measure for he was to be active in the society for years to come. Mike was appointed secretary and had to buy a typewriter for the occasion. After a long discussion it was decided to take out an advert in *The Railway Magazine* and there was some doubt as to whether it was right for them to spend money sent to buy a locomotive to pay for an advert. They went ahead and took the rather bold – not to say rather cheeky – decision to rename themselves. It was at this stage that Frank was co-opted on again. One has to remember that these were all still teenagers and Frank remembers one winter meeting, when they got into a snowball fight that got a bit out of hand and almost caused a rift among the young committee members.

The first meeting of the grandly named 'Great Western Preservation Society' was fixed for the evening of 4 May 1962 at the Southall Community Centre. Angus had reached the age when he could drive and had acquired an Austin 7, which he used to bring a collection of photos, nameplates and number plates to decorate the hall. He was supposed to chair the meeting, but fell ill with appendicitis, and Mike Peart had to step in. He tried to look as grown up as possible in grey flannel school trousers and his father's sports jacket, but was understandably nervous, when faced with a room full of adults. In the event, the evening was to prove a great success and some important new members were introduced, including Edward Boxall, Peter Lemar, Eric Pascoe and Ken Williams, all of whom brought experience of the adult world and each of them would have a stint as chairman. The Society no longer depended entirely on teenagers.

On 1 June that year, the very first Newsletter appeared, price 3d – or 1p in decimal currency - but free to members. The first news item reported that the membership had now reached the very respectable figure of eighty and the funds had reached over a hundred pounds, not a bad start for the infant organisation. The suggestion made in the original letter was that they might also consider acquiring a 'pull-and-push coach'. So as well as hoping to buy a locomotive in good order, they were now looking for a pre-war autocoach, also known as an auto-trailer. This item of rolling stock was developed by the GWR for push-pull trains. The autocoach has a driver's cab at one end. On reaching the end of a branch line,

A reunion of the founding members at Didcot in 1986.

The Society's first locomotive 1466 being inspected at Taunton by Peter Lamar.

instead of having to run the engine round the train for the return journey, the driver would get out and walk down to the cab at the front of the autocoach. From here he could still control the essentials – regulator, brakes and whistle, via a linkage through the coach to an appropriate locomotive – in this case it would be the 14xx. It must have been an interesting experience for the driver who, for the first time in his working life, was presented with a completely clear view of the whole line ahead, rather than having to peer down the side of the boiler. The fireman, of course, had to stay on the footplate, where apart from his normal duties he also controlled the valve settings. Communication between fireman and driver was via a system of electric bells that also connected to the guard; one ring for start, two for stop and three for blow the brakes off. This system using conventional locomotives, adapted for use with an auto-trailer was an adaptation of an earlier system, which will be discussed in Chapter 5.

A few words in the Newsletter suggested that the Society was aware of one problem they would face. It is all very well buying a locomotive and rolling stock – but where do you put them once you've got them? So at the end of the wish list was a simple statement of intent – acquire a branch line. There was a strong hint that something positive might be in the offing – 'but all I am allowed to say at the moment is that vital news should be available in our next issue'. It was certainly becoming vital as they were also discussing acquiring one or more Dean clerestory coaches from BR. Sadly, when the next Newsletter appeared, it was only to report that the hoped-for branch line agreement had vanished. The end of the year did, however, see one change. British Rail in particular were deeply suspicious of anything connected with the word 'preservation' which for them appears to have conjured up a picture of incompetent amateurs running amok all over their rail system. So the word was dropped, and the new name was simply Great Western Society and so it has remained.

Good news appeared in March 1964. Not only had they raised the £750 needed to buy a 14xx but there was somewhere to put it, thanks to one of the members who had attended the inaugural meeting, Peter Lemar. He was an architect based in Torbay, and through his connections heard of a likely site at Totnes. A cattle market had been established on the quay beside the River Dart in the town, and sidings added for moving the stock by rail. But then a decision was taken that no cattle trucks would be used anywhere west of Exeter, so the sidings had become redundant. The construction company now on site had no interest in them, so they

The other item on the first wish list was an autocoach, that would traditionally have been used in conjunction with 1466, and this example from 1951 was soon acquired.

were happy for the GWS to move in. It was just in time, for the Society was now ready to purchase their chosen engine, 1466, which was then delivered to the Totnes site.

In April of that year, four of the old friends crammed into Angus's car to travel down to Totnes to see the engine. He had upgraded, if that is the word, to a Ford Anglia and they arrived at Torquay in time to have lunch with Peter Lemar, who had negotiated the purchase. Having come such a long way, it seemed a shame just to stand around the stationary locomotive, so they decided to raise steam. They gathered together some firewood and Angus claimed that, as he had driven a 5-inch gauge steam locomotive, he should be able to manage a full-sized one. Frank Dumbleton had been given an old sheet to cut up into cleaning rags. Now they tore it apart,

The unofficial inauguration ceremony took place at Totnes when 1466 was steamed and driven through the improvised tape.

knotted the pieces together and tied the resulting line between two gateposts. They then drove 1466 through the 'ceremonial tape' and unofficially inaugurated the first steam run by a GWS locomotive.

There was to be another visit to the south-west the following month and this time they looked in on the Laira Depot at Plymouth, where they discovered 1363, scheduled for scrap. It should already have gone, but due to a damaged buffer beam it was temporarily stuck in the shed. Popular rumour has it that the damage was done 'accidentally on purpose' to save it from being cut up in the hope someone would come along and rescue it. It is an interesting little engine that, in spite of an 0-6-0 wheel configuration, has a short wheel base. This made it ideal for hauling heavy loads where sharp curves were involved. Based on an earlier nineteenth century design for the Cornwall Mineral Railway, No 1363, this later example built in 1910 was among the last group of saddle tanks ever built for the GWR. Once news of its availability got out, a group of members clubbed together to buy it for the Society, and it remains the oldest original GWR locomotive in the collection. The expedition proved to be a success in other ways. The group set off to explore the Exe Valley line, already closed by British Rail, and all kinds of artefacts were just lying around. No one had set up a process for buying bits of abandoned railway, and, as it seemed almost criminal just to leave them lying around, the boot of the Anglia was soon full, and the chassis practically down to the axles. Perhaps some of the mature members might have been more circumspect, but the young men were not quite so fussy.

Railway preservation is sometimes thought of as a strictly male preserve, but that is certainly not true of the GWS. One of the earliest and most enthusiastic members was Viv Cooper and she remembers visits to Totnes, where she had to rough it like everyone else. She joined a working party going down to Totnes for the May Bank Holiday. By this time, the Society had acquired a Dreadnought coach. Built to a Churchward design in 1905, this venerable nine-compartment third class carriage had only survived because it had been used as a dormitory for catering staff. Now it was a dormitory again, but also a store for all kinds of bits and pieces. Viv remembers noticing that if she fell out of her bunk, she'd land on a con rod. It was not exactly ideal, and for later visits they went for the comparative luxury of a B&B.

One of the main objectives of the Society from its foundation had been to have engines that could work out on the track. In the early

1466 fully restored and painted in appropriate GWR livery.

days, however, British Rail were wholly opposed to the idea of any form of steam on their lines, especially steam run by amateurs. Thanks to Doctor Beeching, however, several branch lines had been closed and there was always the possibility of acquiring one as a running line. The process had already started in the south-west, where the Dart Valley Railway was planning to run a steam tourist line, recreating the atmosphere of the original of GWR days. Many in the GWS saw this as an opportunity to use their existing locomotives and rolling stock in an appropriate way and on a former GWR route as well. There was, however, a fundamental difference between the two organisations. The Dart Valley had been conceived first and foremost as a business proposition, which would be required to make a profit for shareholders. There was no intrinsic problem, for the Dart Valley certainly meant to run a genuine heritage railway, but it was quite different from the GWS, the latter being reliant entirely on volunteers and enthusiasts, and only needing sufficient money at this stage to cover their conservation ideas and plans. The differences, however, did not at first seem insurmountable. The proposal was for two separate companies; the Dart Valley

Light Railway Co. to operate the line and the Museum Company, which would look after locomotives and rolling stock not actually owned by Dart Valley and would collect smaller items of railway and transport interest to put on display. There would also be a third organisation, the Dart Valley Railway Association Ltd., which would be a support group made up of enthusiasts, who would be doing volunteer work. There was also a proposal that the locomotive 1466 and the autocoach should be sold to Dart Valley, either for cash or company shares. It was decided to ballot members to get their opinion. Although a considerable number feared being swallowed whole, the majority voted for a closer involvement.

It soon became clear, however, that the Dart Valley was more interested in the hardware than the people, and although the idea of selling off GWS stock was clearly not acceptable, the idea of loans could at least be considered. This would satisfy one of the main objectives of the Society; not simply to preserve historic locomotives and rolling stock, but also to see them in use. Relations were, however, to be sorely tested when the GWS ran an excursion down to Totnes to provide members with the opportunity to see what had been acquired. The intention had been to steam 1466 at Totnes and members would have had the option to stop off at Totnes for the occasion or carry on to Plymouth for a dockyard tour. At the last minute, the Dart Valley got worried about the effects on neighbours of having a steaming so close to the town centre, and if there were objections they could have an effect on their current efforts to get a Light Railways Order. They agreed that the Society would be able to steam the engine but insisted that boiler pressure must not exceed 30psi, which was, of course, entirely useless. Then they had a new idea: they would steam the engine themselves on the now disused branch line to Buckfastleigh. Viv Cooper was on that trip – on the footplate in spite of objections by certain males on the day that it was unlucky to have women on the footplate! She remembers the line as being very overgrown, as no one had cut back any of the line side trees, so that it was all rather like steaming through a dense forest. She actually got hit on the head by a lashing branch – which was then taken as proof that it really was bad luck to have a female person on the engine, a ludicrous notion that has long been disproved by many women volunteers on many different lines.

The outcome of all this was that the volunteers at Totnes had nothing to show anyone and no visitors – and to add insult to injury,

Mike Sanderson, Joe Carter and friends at Taplow.

the Society was blamed for allowing the run on the line without official permission from British Rail. There was, not surprisingly, a great fuss over this unauthorised run, and a subsequent excursion to fetch rolling stock, but although GWS members were involved it was never carried out as an official Society excursion nor given any sort of Society approval. It did nothing to improve relations with Dart Valley. Ultimately, the whole idea of uniting the two concerns was to be quietly dropped.

The collection was growing; the 0-6-0 saddle tank 1363 which had originally been purchased by an independent group was given to the Society, and it was later joined by 1369, which was privately owned. There was a more ambitious plan in hand for a new purchase. The idea was put to the annual general meeting of January 1965 and the management committee was given the go ahead to come up with a plan of action. They decided to look at where there were gaps in the list of locomotives already marked out for preservation and decided that the most obvious omission was the group of 2-cylinder, outside cylinder mixed traffic locomotives, which comprised the 48XX, Saints, Manors, Halls, Granges and the two County classes. The Saints no longer existed, there were no small Counties, no 48XX available and only one steamable large County. The choice came down to a Grange, a Manor or a Hall. Footplate crews liked the Grange engines, but those available proved too expensive. That brought the choice down to two, and there was little to choose in price between the Manors and the Halls. There was, however, a lot to be said in favour of the Hall, a direct descendant of the iconic Saints, developed as early as 1924. It was also felt that with its large tender it would be a contrast to any later member of that group that might be bought later. The question was – which Hall to choose. At this stage it was still being considered in terms of finding a home on the Dart Valley, where it would mainly be seen as a static exhibit, though there was always the possibility of main line running if there was a change of heart at BR. It was decided to ballot the members, who were given the final word on the subject, though in setting out the alternatives in the document sent out to members, the Committee were certainly making their own preferences clear.

'The only suitable original "Hall" is No 6923 "Croxteth Hall", the modified "Halls" are nos. 6959 "Peatling Hall", 6998 "Burton Agnes Hall" and 7924 "Thornycroft Hall". No 6959 was the prototype "Modified Hall" but ran originally with no cabside

The original
Society offices at West Ealing.

windows, nameless and painted black. No 6998 is, without doubt, the best of all, having run only 25,000 miles since heavy general overhaul. It was not built until BR days, and whilst this will be felt by some to be unfortunate, we would point out that the locomotive is of thoroughbred Great Western design, and would have been completed by the G.W. anyway. It may be expected to give three times the life of the others before complete overhaul. This is the loco recommended by the Management Committee.'

A fund was set up and *Burton Agnes Hall* was indeed purchased and agreement was reached with BR that allowed it a triumphant run under its own power from the sheds at Oxford to Totnes Quay on 2 April 1966.

Space was at a premium at Totnes but there was a real enthusiasm developing within the Society, and expansion was, it seems, inevitable. All the time new projects were coming up and although by the start of 1964 membership had risen to over 200, money was still short. While it was possible to raise money for locomotives, it was always more difficult to get cash for coaches, even though they were considerably cheaper. But somehow, £300 had been found to buy an autocoach. After that, the coffers were more or less empty, yet cash still had to be found for essentials such as insurance. So when new and very desirable locomotives became available, there was a dilemma, which was partly solved by individual members making private purchases. Mike Higson had mentioned that he was interested in buying a Black 5 but was persuaded to look instead at purchasing *Pendennis Castle*. It can be a tricky business, combining a society's interests with those of the private owner, and that proved to be the case. The engine was duly bought and brought to Swindon for overhaul. Ken Williams was at that time Chair of the Society and wanted to claim expenses for working on the Castle. But it was not going to be owned by the Society, so the request was turned down, at which point he resigned and Eric Pascoe took over. The Castle departed but was, however, to turn up again many years later.

It was not just locomotives that were being purchased, but more coaches were also being added to the collection. There was another problem in that with almost everything based at Totnes, all the necessary maintenance and restoration work fell on that branch – and there was a serious shortage of volunteers available locally. Add to that, the fact that there was a mere quarter of a mile of

running track, and there was an obvious need for an alternative if the Society was going to expand.

The Society had already begun spawning branches and one of these, based in Reading, began seriously to investigate the idea that space might be made available at Taplow, where there was a disused siding. This station has an interesting history. The first station was actually the eastern terminus for the Great Western while the viaduct was being constructed at Maidenhead and was actually known either as Maidenhead or Maidenhead Riverside. Once the line was open across the river, the little station lost its temporary importance and a new station was built at the present site, though some distance from the village. No one was about to divert the line to serve the small community. Today's main line expresses whisk through at high speed so that most passengers are scarcely aware of its existence. It does, however, still enjoy a regular if infrequent service by decidedly slower stopping trains. In general, at this time, the attitude of management at BR was that everything possible should be done to modernise the system, and say goodbye to steam forever, which they regarded as now representing a form of transport that might have been revolutionary in the nineteenth century but was totally inappropriate for the second half of the

6106 taking on water before setting off from Southall.

Cookham Manor with an admiring crowd at the 1966 Taplow Open Day.

twentieth. The more zealous were all for sweeping away the past altogether, but some realised that the steam age had played a vital role in developing modern civilisation around the world, and it was in Britain that it had all begun. They sympathised with those who were striving to preserve this vital heritage. Fortunately, among that enlightened band was David Pattison, the manager of Western Division, who was happy to see the Society take space at Taplow.

A member had privately purchased No 6106, a 2-6-2T built at Swindon in 1931, and it had been given a home at Taplow. News that a steam locomotive was based in the yard by the station reached two teenage schoolboys, Mike Sanderson and Joe Carter, who strolled along to take a look and, to their surprise, found the engine in steam and not a soul in sight. They resisted the temptation to drive it away and came back later where they met T.W.E. Roche and when the boys indicated they would like to get involved he handed them oily rags and told them to get going. Inevitably, given his initials, he was always known as Twee to the boys, who recruited friends to join in the activities. They remember him as a good organiser, but not necessarily an expert on railways and locomotives. A certain amount of resourcefulness was needed in those early days. Before the arrival of a coach with a kitchen, cooking consisted of putting food in a bucket and heating it with a blowlamp. By the time there was a large gang at work, their breaks were lengthened by only having a small teapot to serve them all, which required constant refilling. A vast brown, enamelled pot soon appeared, known as the Twee pot. But when it came to ordering coal for the locomotive he was less successful, simply ordering coal suitable for a domestic boiler – what they got was anthracite, which burns at far too high a temperature – the boys had a long job cleaning up the fire grate after a run. It was also hard work coaling, as the fuel was dumped at ground level, then had to be shovelled up onto the footplate and from there into the bunker. The Society was anxious to show off its wares but was understandably nervous about the expense involved in setting up large open days. The first was for members and friends and the Newsletter urged everyone to make an effort to turn up. In the event, far greater numbers appeared than they had ever imagined. It was an encouraging sign for the future.

The event that really demonstrated that the Society could attract the general public was the grand open day held at Taplow in September 1966. It was held in co-operation with British Rail, who had their own exhibition train and a cinema coach on display. The Society had acquired three of the magnificent Ocean saloons,

Burton Agnes Hall at Taplow.

built at Swindon in the 1930s, when Charles Benjamin Collett was the chief mechanical engineer. They were designed to take passengers from Paddington to Plymouth, which was then one of the main ports used by transatlantic liners. Being high prestige vehicles, they were given appropriately royal names as well as mere numbers – the three owned by the GWS were *Queen Mary*, *Queen Elizabeth* and the *Prince of Wales*. Visitors could take trips in 9112 *Queen Mary*, hauled by No 6106. Later in the day, *Pendennis Castle* arrived and was available for inspection. The day was given an official opening by the Mayor of Reading and 2,000 paid to come to the event, later followed by another 200 who arrived on a special from Birmingham hauled by *Cookham Manor*. This was an exhilarating run, with the old engine achieving speeds of up to 80mph. It was all a startling contrast with previous open days at Totnes Quay, when less than a hundred appeared. A second open day was arranged for the following year, but without British Rail involvement, as by this time they wanted nothing to do with

Taplow visitors were supposed to have had a temporary platform for boarding the train but in its absence, they had to use a short stepladder to clamber into the *Prince of Wales* coach.

steam. However, the British Transport Cinema, housed in a former LNWR 12-wheeled coach from the 1900s, put in an appearance. The star attractions were a Collett 0-6-0 tender goods from the Severn Valley Railway and 4079 *Pendennis Castle* which had been bought from scrap in 1964 by Mike Higson. It was an outstanding success and a great encouragement to keep moving forward, but the same problem of space for expansion had yet to be solved.

By this time, the Society had reorganised its affairs to formulate two separate companies. The first was to be the Great Western Society Ltd., which would carry on the work of the Society and incorporate all its main aims and would include provision for membership and for establishing different branches. To simplify the changeover, the first Council of Management would consist of the former Management Committee. There would then be a Stock Company. While the Society Company would be open to anyone who wanted to join who shared its general aim, the Stock Company would be limited to fifty shareholders, though it was assumed they would also be Society members. This company was to have responsibility for looking after all the locomotives and rolling stock, and, when appropriate, run or help to run any branch line that might be acquired, apply for any necessary light railway orders and generally keep things running. It made a lot of sense to separate out the admin side of the Society, who would be responsible for such matters as finance and the everyday work of restoration and running. It would, however, be unfair to think of this in very simple terms; a lot of pen pushers on one hand and oil can wielders on the other. The Society has never worked like that, and it is certainly not the case that Society Board members never get their hands dirty; it is, after all, the love of the railway itself that unites everyone. It is simply a fact of life that the separation is necessary for any organisation to work efficiently.

Taplow had many advantages over Totnes but was still far from perfect as a permanent headquarters. Although the Society had use of the shed, the yard was still used for storing rolling stock – and any time a locomotive had to be run, they all had to be shunted out of the way to clear a long enough section of track. There was also a problem with water supply. A hydrant had been located, but when it was put to use there were angry complaints from locals who found they were only getting a dribble out of their domestic taps. Fortunately, there was a large house nearby with an outside tap, and the owners agreed to it being used. But the house was at the

6106 arriving at Olympia to collect coaches.

end of a long drive, so whenever a locomotive needed filling, there had to be enough water in the boiler to drive it to the nearest point. Even then, a long hosepipe was needed and a complete refill of the tender tank took many hours. It was by then already clear that there was not going to be a lasting relationship with Dart Valley, so when an offer was made to make space available at Didcot depot, it was enthusiastically accepted. At this stage, the depot was still being used for BR Western Division diesels, and *Flying Scotsman* had also found a temporary home there. The big plus factor was that the site had a great potential for development. There was also a hint that having steam so close to the main line at Taplow was irritating the authorities, especially those who wanted to see the end of steam and did not wish to have a constant reminder in such a prominent position. So stock began to arrive at the Didcot depot.

Among items that needed to be moved were two coaches, one of which, the brake car *Isle of Thanet*, was of considerable historical significance as it had made up part of the funeral train that had brought Sir Winston Churchill's body from London to Hanborough; a train headed very appropriately by a Battle of Britain class locomotive. Ironically, the date chosen for collection was just one week after the Western Region had announced that no more steam trains were to run on their rails. Not only was 6106 to be used for the journey, running light into London, but it would steam into the station at Olympia Kensington, then having to serve as the London terminus while extensive modernisation was being carried out at Paddington. Among other historically interesting rolling stock collected at about this time were the sleeping carriages from General Eisenhower's Second World War train. On the journey to collect this rolling stock, several people expressed an enthusiastic interest in coming along for the ride, including a clergyman. He was invited onto the footplate and it was only when they had got under way that the crew finally realised just who they had on board – a gentleman who had probably done more to interest children in railways than anyone else, the Rev W. Awdry.

Having locomotives and stock spread over three centres was clearly not ideal. The Society was spurred into action when they received a strong hint from David Pattison that, because he was leaving his current job to take a seat on the Board of BR, there might

The move from Totnes to Didcot, with *Burton Agnes Hall* leading the way, followed by 1466 and the Society's coaches.

not be an opportunity under new management to take steam trains from Totnes to Didcot. That decided the issue: everything would come to Didcot. The epic journey began on 1 December 1967. *Burton Agnes Hall* and No 1466 were sent with the Collett all third coach no.5292, Dreadnought third No 3299, the auto trailer No 3299 and a British Rail BG full of spares to Laira for inspection before they were allowed out on the tracks. It had been agreed that passengers could be carried on the trip, so a hundred Society members came along for the ride. The next day, they started out on the journey. As darkness fell, an attempt was made to light the carriages, in the hope that enough power had been generated for the electrics to work. Switching on produced an alarming cloud of blue smoke, so the attempt was hurriedly abandoned. Some of the passengers had brought along Tilly lamps that provided a flickering light for the reminder of the journey, though whether the authorities would have ever authorised the use of naked flames in wooden carriages is another matter. They finally arrived late in the evening.

With the journey completed and with no stock remaining at Taplow, the Society now had a home. Didcot was the new base and would remain so right up to the present day, though it was to change a great deal over the coming years. The Society was to develop in all kinds of directions never even dreamed of by the schoolboy originators, including a reconstruction of the early days of broad gauge travel, none of which would have been possible without that decision having been taken. The Society had the foresight to recognise Didcot's potential and over the years that potential would be realised.

CHAPTER THREE

Locomotives

The Society had its origins in the desire to preserve one particular class of steam locomotive, but as it developed over the years a more ambitious target was set. It was decided to put together a collection that would show the development of GWR steam locomotives of the standard gauge era of all types, from the humblest shunting engine to the mightiest main line express. That it has succeeded is a remarkable achievement. Visitors to the site can see a fine array of locomotives up close and on steam days ride behind one or more of them. What they do not see is the huge effort that goes into bringing these engines back to life, many of which were rescued from the famous scrap yard on Barry Island. It is unnecessary to go into details of every single restoration job, but one locomotive stands out as having a very special and unusual history and having been subject to a long, careful and expensive restoration process – No 4079 *Pendennis Castle*.

Pendennis Castle fully restored with a vintage directors' saloon.

The Star class introduced at the beginning of the twentieth century by the chief mechanical engineer George Jackson Churchward had been very successful, a 4-cylinder 4-6-0 that incorporated a number of key features, especially the long-travel valves and the Belpaire firebox. The latter was not exactly new, having been developed in Belgium in 1864, but it was far more efficient than any earlier firebox. It has a broad, flat top section that allows for maximum evaporation of water into steam. By the 1920s, the need for an improved, more powerful engine was becoming pressing. C.B. Collett had taken over as chief engineer from Churchward and he set about making significant changes to the basic Star design. The frame was extended and a large, lighter No 8 boiler was used. With more steam available, it was possible to increase cylinder size from 15x25ins to 16x26ins. The engineer was sufficiently confident to order ten of the class in 1923 and one of these was *Pendennis Castle*, completed in 1924.

The first of the new class 'Caerphilly Castle' was sent to the British Empire Exhibition at Wembley in 1924, where it stood close to another giant of the day, the pride of the LNER's A3 Pacifics, *Flying Scotsman*. Inevitably, comparisons were being made, each company claiming superiority for their own machine. It was decided to put the matter to the test in a set of trials in 1925. To ensure that any performance was unaffected by the track, it was decided to have two sets of locomotives, one running on the GWR and the other on the LNER. The honour of carrying the colours for the Great Western on northern rails went to *Pendennis Castle*. The engine performed remarkably well on the run from King's Cross to Doncaster, coping

King Edward II
at Barry scrap yard – because of the condition, the locomotive had to be taken apart and moved in sections for restoration.

with a heavy train and negotiating the tricky, steep climb out of London with ease. The locomotive continued to give good service for many years until it was eventually retired and bought by Sir Robert McAlpine. When the GWS arrived at Didcot, their locomotives shared the shed with McAlpine's Castle and his other acquisition – *Flying Scotsman*. The two famous locomotives were side by side again after a gap of almost half a century.

The story now moves across the globe to Australia. A group of workers, who had originally worked on railways in Britain before leaving to take jobs at Hamersley Iron in Western Australia, persuaded the management that it would be a good idea to run a steam locomotive on their freight line, just for pleasure. They set their sets high; they decided *Flying Scotsman* would be ideal, but McAlpine had no intention of selling. As he later remarked, if he'd allowed that iconic engine to go out to a new home across the world he was in serious danger of facing a railway enthusiast lynch mob. But he was prepared to sell *Pendennis Castle* – even if to many enthusiasts that engine has every much a right to star status as the *Scotsman*. So off to Australia the engine went in 1977. It ran until 1984, was given a complete boiler overhaul and was back on the tracks. She then ran again from 1987-94. Because of the intense heat of the Western Australian desert, excursions were limited to the winter months. At the end of that running season, the locomotive was laid up and it was decided not to carry out any more major repairs and overhauls. Instead, the company offered it free of charge to Didcot. It sounds an extraordinary bargain, but there was a catch; the society would have to pay the cost of bringing her home.

Richard Antliff, the Society's Civil Engineering Manager, was in Australia when the offer was made and he began planning for the repatriation. He had considerable experience of working in the Far East and was familiar with the general costs of using container ships. He estimated that the price was likely to be in the region of £40,000. The first obvious stop was P&O, who had shipped the engine out to Australia in the first place. They came back with a quote of delivering her to a port in the Mediterranean for £125,000. It was time to think again, and Richard thought of a very ambitious notion – why not use one of the huge Russian Antonov freight planes? It was an intriguing idea – making a castle in the air into a reality. They could do it – but their bill was an astronomical £360,000. Repatriation was starting to look prohibitively expensive.

At this point he was contacted by a gentleman in East Anglia, who wrote to say that he thought he might be able to help. He had used a freight forwarder who had brought a tram back from Portugal – not quite the same as a locomotive from Australia but it sounded promising. Just two weeks later the news came through that the problem was solved; he had found a round the world ferry that would collect the locomotive from Melbourne. Unfortunately, the Castle was 2,500 miles away on the other side of the continent. Richard asked if there was any chance of the locomotive being collected from Perth. The answer came back, yes it can be picked up from there and delivered to Avonmouth for £41,000 – almost exactly what Richard had estimated in the first place. Fund raising had already got well under way, and the offer was at once accepted.

The locomotive now had to be driven about 1,000 miles from Dampier on the north coast of Western Australia to Perth. The trip took 36 hours and at the end there was a formal handing over ceremony between Rio Tinto, who now controlled Hamersley and Richard Antliff and the Society's General Manager, Mick Dean. The two Brits had the pleasure of riding through the streets of Perth on *Pendennis Castle* in the company of an anxious man with a long pole, making sure that the chimney didn't foul any of the overhead electric wires. There was one amusing incident when a large 4x4 drew up and an official looking gentleman got out, put on his white hard hat and marched purposely towards the locomotive. Richard Antliff's first thought was that he was going to announce a problem with the paperwork or some other bureaucratic difficulty. Instead of which his first words were, 'Do you know Peter Lamar?' It was then established that he had joined the GWS in Taunton at almost exactly the same time as Richard – their membership numbers were 396 and 402. There was no problem there, but another difficulty soon appeared.

Arrangements had been made for the locomotive to be placed on a low loader for transport back to England and a specialist company, Brambles, had been given the job. The dockers, however, insisted it was their job. After a great deal of argument, a compromise was reached: Brambles would load the locomotive, the dockers the tender. In the event, the complex job of loading the locomotive was completed two and a half hours before the tender was loaded. At last, the long journey home could begin. It was not exactly a speedy return as the ship travelled over to the west coast

A triumph for the restorers: *King Edward II* returned to former glory.

of America, through the Panama Canal, and then up to Canada before finally crossing the Atlantic and arriving in England after an 80-day voyage. The locomotive finally arrived home in July 2000.

Now the long process of restoration could begin. What always has to be remembered when looking at projects such as this is that a vast amount of work is done by volunteers in their spare time. Even the current head of the project, Drew Ferman, has a full-time job as a teacher. The first essential was to find out what needed to be done and that meant stripping everything out, bringing the whole machine right down to the frames and giving everything a thorough clean. There was immediate evidence of where she had been run for the last few years as buckets full of red desert sand were removed. The good news was that the boiler, while requiring some work, was in reasonably good condition. Partly this was due to the fact that the Australians had taken good care of the engine while it was in their care, and partly due to a fortunate circumstance. The water in Western Australia has a high mineral content that can be very injurious to all kinds of machines, including steam engines. The company needed to purify it for use with their own machinery and installed a reverse osmosis plant that produces a very pure water, almost as pure as distilled water. This water was available for use in the locomotive boiler. Then, after each run, the boiler was drained. Normally, a certain amount of water collects in nooks and

The former Wantage tramway locomotive *Shannon* being collected from Culham for transport to Didcot.

crannies, where it can mix with other materials to form an acidic, mildly corrosive mixture. But in the heat of the Australian desert it all rapidly evaporated leaving the boiler bone dry. This was a very welcome discovery.

Once everything was stripped down, and all the grime removed, it was possible to assess exactly what needed to be done; dirt can hide an awful lot of flaws and cracks. Not surprisingly with a locomotive of this age, there was a great deal of wear. This was made even worse by the conditions in which it had been run for the last few years. When the desert sand got mixed with any leaking oil, it formed an excellent grinding paste. The tyres on the locomotive were a bit rough and will need to be turned – a job still waiting to be done. This will have to be done by an outside contractor, as Didcot does not have a big enough lathe. The wheels on the tender, however, were very bad indeed. Fortunately, there was a complete set of tender wheels available in store that could be used for replacements. The wheels that had been removed were now available for retyring for another project at a later date. Now, some people might think that not having the original in place somehow makes the whole machine less than original. In fact, the workers at Didcot will use original material as far as possible, but there has to be a balance struck between the desire to be responsible curators and engineering necessity. In any case, they are only doing what was being done at Swindon when the locomotives were in service. The 4079 that arrived back at Didcot was already substantially different from the 4079 that left Swindon works. It would almost certainly have needed a new boiler at some time and there is direct evidence of change when one looks at the locomotive in detail. Inspecting the motion, you will find engraved numbers on parts such as slide bars and connecting rods. One number will be that of the locomotive itself. But at some stage it has come in for repair and that part would have needed machining. Instead of keeping the locomotive standing idle, waiting for the work to be completed, another identical part from another locomotive of the same class could be fitted. It would have its original number engraved and now the new number would be added. When the engine went to Australia and had to run in hot desert conditions, it was found to be necessary to change the injectors to adjust to the extreme climate. Back at Didcot, these had to be replaced to restore the locomotive

The restored *Shannon* on show at Didcot.

to its original condition, and to allow for the change from hot, steamy desert to cool, damp Britain. By a happy coincidence, GWR injectors were available that had originally belonged to number 4074, which was *Caldicot Castle*, the other locomotive that had taken part in the 1925 trials.

There was a lot of work that needed doing. Many bearing surfaces had to be machined, but there was a nasty surprise when it came to inspecting the cylinders and smoke box saddle, made up of four cast iron sections. A section at the rear of the saddle carries the exhaust pipes down to the outside cylinders, and these are bolted to a flange. That turned out to have a large crack in it. A twelve-inch section had to be carefully taken out, a difficult job in itself, and sent away for welding. It took two or three days to get all the bolts out and another day, working with jacks and a crane, to remove the whole section. Didcot can weld steel but cast iron presents a very special problem, as it first has to be brought to a very high temperature and then cooled slowly to avoid causing fresh cracks in the iron. Once it was returned, it proved almost equally difficult to put back in place, There was no rush to do this, as with this large block of metal out of the way it was much easier to get at the motion and valves.

Work had to be done on the valves. Where metal has worn away, modern technology allows it to be replaced, using a technique known as spiral welding – another job that has to go to specialists. New valve and cylinder linings were put in, which altered the dimensions. Valve heads from Swindon came in two sizes, A and B. Originally, 4074 was fitted with the larger B heads but now had to come down to the slightly smaller A heads, which came from 5051 *Drysllwyn Castle* – a locomotive that also supplied the eccentrics. The metal panels on the cab and tender proved a problem. Coal dust and water tend to collect at the bottom of panels, forming a corrosive mixture that eats away at the metal. New platework had to be ordered and welded in. The welds are all but invisible from the outside but can be seen on the inside. This is deliberate; it shows the history of the overhaul in the physical record. There is, however, equal care taken to ensure that even the smallest historic detail is preserved if possible. For example, in British Rail days there were clips on the cab side to which the driver's name was added. They are being kept in place, even though only a few will appreciate their significance. Sometimes it was thought more appropriate to take the engine back a stage. Some of the pipework had been altered in Australia and that was brought back to its original condition.

The state of play in the summer of 2017 was that the boiler was almost completely renovated, but further restoration had been put on hold. The locomotive had been in bits since 2000, and now it was essential to see that everything that needed to be done had been done and everything was present and correct. To do so, it was necessary to put the incomplete boiler back in the frame and start the job of reassembly. Once everything is back in place and can be seen to fit together ready for action, it all has to be removed, carefully labelled and stored – a Castle construction kit. Then the boiler can be removed, the work finished and it can be given its hydraulic test and, with luck, receive its certificate. At the time of writing, *Pendennis Castle* had been reassembled and looked magnificent. One item was missing, however, that was about to be added. The solid brass nameplate was safely stored away in the museum and would be attached when the engine went on show at the end of August to coincide with her old stable mate *Flying Scotsman*, due to visit Didcot. Eventually, when the locomotive goes

The work crew posing during restoration work on 5051.

back into service, she will be fitted with a replica nameplate – you can tell the difference when you lift them up. Instead of the heavy solid brass lettering of the original, lettering on the replica is hollow, but they look absolutely identical. Nobody is going to leave the engine standing around with the extremely valuable original in place. A classic nameplate such as this could fetch £60,000 or more if it came on the market.

The big question obviously is – when will *Pendennis Castle* be completed and steam again? No one is going to answer at this stage. There are two very good reasons. Restoration is a slow, careful process and nobody knows in advance exactly what problems might occur. It is better not to speculate than to give a date that it turns out can't be met for unforeseen reasons. Then again, it always has to be remembered that most of the work falls to volunteers who freely give their time, because the job is worth doing and because they enjoy doing it. What they don't need is the pressure of deadlines to be met. The way of working may seem slow, but it is steady and careful. The locomotive has been around for almost a hundred years and everyone wants to ensure that it survives for many more decades – and who knows, one day they might be celebrating the bicentenary. If that happens it will be down to the good work and care taken by the volunteers, first out in Australia and then at home in Didcot.

There are certain times of the year when Didcot is especially busy – the work weeks, when large numbers of volunteers get together. Visiting on such a day gives a really good idea of the variety of work that goes on, a lot of which is very far from glamorous. Patiently rubbing down a locomotive ready for a new coat of paint, for example, is tedious but essential – but the volunteers at work that day on that very task seemed happy and cheerful. I was given a tour of the locomotives and workshops by Drew Ferman, and this description of what I saw is probably fairly typical – but on a different day work would have been carried out perhaps on quite different locomotives and very different tasks would have been involved. It was also an opportunity to look at some of the fascinating details that make each exhibit unique. Not all the locomotives in the collection are necessarily on site at any one time – some are out on loan to other preservation railways. A list of all the locomotives in the historic collection is given in the appendix and where there is no description in the main text, extra information has been added.

The all-important hydraulic boiler test, being carried out on 6998, that has to be passed before the locomotive can be steamed.

Going out on the site on a working week, the most obviously striking feature is the rather eerie screech made by the shunting diesel, moving stock around. One locomotive, No 4144, had been taken out of the shed so that work could be done, and parts of the motion had already been removed with the help of a portable jack that had begun its working life at Swindon. This 2-6-2T engine, built in 1946, worked for a long time as a banker at the Severn tunnel. This is one of those hard-working engines that don't necessarily attract much attention, but have a long history, being developed from a Churchward design from the beginning of the twentieth century and gradually changed and given different classifications, from the original 45xx through to this 51xx and on to 61xx, 31xx and 81xx. This is the mark of a successful engine, and it has proved a popular and useful locomotive for the preservation movement. It is powerful but economical in terms of both water and coal. This particular locomotive has a new boiler that came from a 600 class, which enabled steam pressure to be increased from 200 pounds per square inch (psi) to 225psi. This means it can reach its operating speed quite quickly, which is very helpful when you only have a comparatively short running line. With another locomotive, there might only be time to get up to speed before it is time to start slowing down again for the end of the line. 4144 gives a decent run at a reasonable speed.

There are always decisions to be made about livery with an engine that had several masters. When it was last taken out of service for extensive repairs there was inevitably some damage to the paintwork involved in removing and replacing parts. It had been last seen in GWR livery, but it was decided to make a change. The choice fell to putting the engine into British Rail colours, but with a difference. At nationalisation there had been no immediate decision on standardising lettering and logo, so when Swindon were given the task of painting with the new company name, they used the familiar Great Western lettering. The idea behind the change of style at Didcot was that it would please everyone – it

There is one job for which the Society has to call in the experts; a sign painter at work on the tender of 6998.

would show the locomotive as it was in its latter working days, but also provide a reminder of its earlier history as part of a Great Western class. As so often at Didcot, there is a story that is unique to that particular item. On going round the shed looking at other items in the collection, more stories began to emerge. The following descriptions appear in the order in which I visited the different engines. It does not follow a logical sequence, but this is also the way in which visitors meet the different exhibits and to me part of the charm of the experience comes from the variety of finding a little shunting engine nestling up to a main line express.

No 5322 is one of the most fascinating locomotives in the collection. The 43xx Class was first introduced in 1911, but many were converted into Manors and Granges. Conversion was brought to a halt in the First World War. The Army had an urgent need for heavy locomotives to bring supplies from the Channel ports to the front line. The various railway companies were approached and asked to supply locomotives. The GWR pointed out that their 2-8-0s were fully employed carrying coal for the warships of the fleet, and the Navy would take a dim view of their being pinched by the Army. The company pointed out, however, that they could supply 2-6-0s, provided the War Ministry provided the materials. 5322 was one of twenty built in the war years. A serving officer with the Railways Operating Division (ROD) wrote an account of seeing the engine in France that appeared in the *Great Western Echo* in 1973. He was aware of being overtaken by a train on its way from Calais to the front.

'There was no mistaking the type of locomotive – by the beat of its exhaust – a GWR Mogul, thus confirming it was almost certainly one of the 53s doing such splendid work for the Army. She overtook me at the Pont des Briques crossing, with its metal rolling gates, and it was easy to see her number in large white letters on the tender – ROD 5322. Behind her were the customary 44 or so wagons, the supplies for two divisions. The gross load was some 770 tons.'

The locomotive was clearly living up to the promise made by the GWR that a 2-6-0 was capable of doing serious, heavy work. At the end of the war, she was sent to Pontypool and remained at work until 1964, a remarkable story of mechanical endurance. Then she was sent to Barry, but fortunately her importance was recognised before the blow torches began their work and in 1973 she arrived at Didcot. It might be thought that by this time everything that could be known about the locomotive was known, but it seems there is always something left to be discovered. There are clips in the corners of the roof at each side of the cab that nobody thought about very much. It was decided to hold a World War One Day, and the locomotive was painted in a military khaki. Driver and fireman were in uniform and equipped with short magazine Lee Enfield rifles. They then had to think where to put them while at work and that was when they noticed the clips – and they fitted perfectly. During the war, the crew would have been serving soldiers and armed, so those were the original rifle clips, a small detail perhaps but a reminder that train crews in France were every bit as involved in active service as the men in the trenches.

No 7808 *Cookham Manor* was the only Manor to be held by British Rail, and it has physical evidence of its origins in a 43 Class Mogul. Parts remained standardised, so that they could be changed and on one of the connecting rods is the engraved letter 'R' to show it has to be fitted on the right hand side, the present locomotive number and the number of the engine in which it was first used – 5380, the 43 Class. Although one reads in books that the Manors were adapted from 43s, it is still very satisfying to find this actual physical evidence.

No 6998 *Burton Agnes Hall* is known as a modified Hall. The Halls were a highly successful design, satisfying the need for a powerful, general purpose engine and over 300 were built. The original had been designed by Collett, with a prototype appearing in 1924. There were a few minor changes over the years but there was a radical rethinking when Frederick Hawksworth took over in Swindon in 1941. At first sight, the modified Hall looked very much like its predecessor but in fact had several very different features. In the original, the cylinders were cast into the frames but Hawksworth used a plate frame running the length of the engine, with cylinders bolted to the outside. He also replaced the old bar frame on the bogie with a plate frame. The degree of superheating was increased at the same time. It was a very successful engine.

Burton Agnes Hall is very much a Didcot veteran and, after restoration, made her appearance at the open weekend in 1972. She ran mainly on number 8 road with three Collett coaches and was very much the star attraction. At this stage, British Rail still had an interest in the site and put on a display of their own locomotives and rolling stock. Enthusiasts are always impressed by the fact that she still has her original tender. A note on the restoration process gives an idea of the conditions under which the early volunteers had to work. At the end of 1969, the locomotive was given a tent-like covering made of heavy duty polythene sheeting, with heating provided by a space heater and lighting by portable fluorescent tubes. It was felt that this was enough for work to be carried out throughout the winter months.

When a locomotive has the number 1, you might think it would be one of the oldest in the collection, but this little saddle tank engine was built in 1949. It is something of an interloper, having been built

The footplate crew taking a breather beside 3217, on loan from the Bluebell Railway.

by Robert Stephenson & Hawthorns and entered service at Poole Docks, which is where it got the number and a name – *Bonnie Prince Charlie*. A small but powerful engine, it does have one item to remind everyone of its nautical past – instead of the conventional locomotive whistle, this one came off a ship – and has earned the engine the local nickname of 'Tugboat'. She was originally purchased by the Salisbury Locomotive Society in 1969. They had originally hoped to buy a former Southern locomotive, but the price was too high, so they were pleased to hear that *Bonnie Prince Charlie* was available at Dibble Wharf, Southampton. The owner, the coal merchants Corralls, had two other engines available – a former LSWR 0-4-0T and a diesel shunter – so were happy to let one go. The Society agreed that if she steamed and ran satisfactorily they would buy the engine. She passed the test and shortly afterwards arrived at Didcot. It was there during a maintenance test that they discovered why Corrals had decided to keep an engine from the 1890s and sell off a more modern locomotive. The vacuum tubes were full of small coal and coal dust, and the engine could only have hauled a single 20-ton coal truck. Corralls must have been glad to get rid of her for £400.

Another low numbered locomotive really is old. No 5 has had a chequered history, having been built by George England in 1857 for the privately run Sandy & Potten Railway but ending up on the Wantage Tramway, which is where it came into the Great Western family. When the main line was being constructed, it by-passed Wantage, but after complaints from the inhabitants of the market town, a compromise of a sort was reached. A station was opened at Grove, 2½ miles away, and named Wantage Road. For a time, a horse bus provided an inadequate link between town and station, but in 1875 it was supplanted by the steam-powered tramway. It was welcomed by the locals with a poem, damning the old bus and welcoming the railway.

From the station to Wantage an omnibus runs –
A small one – now pray do not laugh,
When I tell you the fare they charge over there
Is a 'bob' for two miles and a half.

They think bye and bye the rail will be nigh,
And then at the bus they will laugh;
They will ride in good style at a penny a mile
And no 'bobs' for two miles and a half.

Younger readers might need to know that a bob was a shilling, twenty to the pound, and there were twelve pennies in a shilling. The venerable locomotive is very basic, with just one injector and the water gauge has no protective cover of any kind. Like all locomotives in the collection it was treated carefully when it arrived. It was rubbed down, and as layers of paintwork disappeared, the original Wantage Tramway lettering began to emerge. It was traced, photographed and then covered in varnish, so that when the locomotive is again sanded down at some future date, the varnish will act as a barrier and prevent this historic link being lost. The intention is to replace the lettering at some future date.

When Wantage Road was closed down, *Jane* was moved to the Atomic Energy Research Establishment at Harwell in 1965. Lyndon Elias, a GWS member, worked there and felt that it was not the best place to preserve the engine. He and his friends persuaded John Scholes, curator of the National Collection, that the engine should be given a new home at Didcot, a spot close to her former working site at Wantage.

This is the last surviving standard gauge locomotive from the England works at New Cross. The company did, however, provide the first locomotives to run on the narrow gauge Ffestiniog Railway in Wales. There is a curious little story here which, though it really has little to do with Didcot, is worth telling. George England employed a young engineer, recently returned from India, called Robert Fairlie. Now, Fairlie is of course famous for the double-ended locomotives that are also preserved on the Ffestiniog, which might lead one to suppose they enjoyed a close relationship – far from it. Fairlie fell for England's 17-year-old daughter Eliza, but England refused to allow them to marry. So the pair eloped and Fairlie rather rashly signed an affidavit to say the father approved the match. When he heard about it, England charged Fairlie with perjury and the case came to court. It was only then that another fact emerged – England was not married to Eliza's mother, and though he lived with her they were unable to marry as he already had a wife. That made Eliza illegitimate, and according to the law of the day, she had no legal parents. So England's permission had never been needed. The case collapsed. The great railway engineers are often looked on as heroes of the day, so it is always good to be reminded that no heroes are ever perfect.

The next engine in the line-up could hardly present a greater contrast – No 5051. Like other Castle class locomotives, she was given an appropriately castellated name – *Drysllwyn Castle* but this was later somewhat confusingly changed to *Earl Bathurst*. It seems that some of the noble directors of the GWR pestered the company to have locomotives named after them. A 'new' class was being developed, known as Duke Dogs, because they used the boilers from old withdrawn Duke Class engines with the frames and running gear from Bulldogs. The first twenty were given 'Earl' names, but these were distinctly old-fashioned looking engines that harked back to the Victorian age. When the assembled directors realised what had happened – and that included the former Prime Minister, now Earl, Baldwin, they were not amused. The name plates were withdrawn and attached to Castles. The locomotive is currently out of service having already done two tickets – that is been approved after two major overhauls. If she's to go back to work, there'll certainly be a great deal to do mechanically and a new tender tank will be needed. If it is decided to put her back into service, then at least all the bits are there. This was certainly not the case, when the engine was bought from Barry. But she deserves a bit of a rest. This is an engine that has worked hard for the Society and was never seen to better effect than on an excursion to Derbyshire in May 1981.

The pannier tank on an unseasonably snowy April day.

The start from Didcot was delayed by seven minutes due to the late arrival of a train from Paddington, bringing many of the excursion passengers. The locomotive had a train made up of eleven carriages, the heaviest load taken by the engine since restoration. With such a load and in pouring rain, the crew must have felt some anxiety about making a clean start, but they set off without a whisper of wheel slip. The next stop was Banbury and before that there was the formidable obstacle of Hatton Bank to overcome, a 2½ mile stretch of line at a ruling gradient of 1 in 105. The Castle stormed up it at a minimum speed of 57mph, a performance that any Great Western crew would have been proud to achieve. She actually arrived at Banbury nine minutes early. There were more delays, caused by hold ups at signals and late running of normal service trains. On the outward journey, the Castle stopped at Tyseley and handed over to diesel for the next stage, and waited for the return, the crew no doubt hoping for better luck. They were to be disappointed. For some unknown reason, the water gauge suddenly shattered. A replacement had to be found, but that failed as well. The crew had no option but to travel without the gauge, having to do what crews on the earliest locomotives would have done – use the two test cocks to measure water levels. Thanks to their perseverance and skill, everyone got home safely. It was what one might describe as an interesting trip.

No 5900 *Hinderton Hall* demonstrated an interesting feature of Swindon practice. White metal for such items as bearings and bronze brushes were passed down the line. If everything was not in good condition on a Hall then these items would have been replaced, but the old ones would not have been thrown away. They moved down from express to mixed traffic to freight, to shunting and only when they were too worn for shunting were they finally thrown away. *Hinderton Hall* has seen quite a few parts removed and replaced down the years. The locomotive has been used in the past at Didcot but is now on static display, joining the queue of locomotives waiting for a refit.

No 6697 is an interesting engine in that it was built for the Great Western, but not to an original GWR design. The various lines that connected the valleys of South Wales were noted for steep gradients and locomotives needed to be able to work hard with heavy loads, but speed was of secondary importance and they never had to make long journeys. Locomotives such as this 0-6-2T were designed for just that job. When the GWR took over the system in 1923, they inherited a set of pretty worn out locomotives, but at the same time they recognised that the existing stock was ideally suited to the conditions. There was no point in redesigning anything – reinventing the wheel – but they needed a lot of engines quite quickly and there was more work than Swindon could handle, so different companies were given the orders. This one was built by Armstrong of Newcastle in 1928.

No 5572 is one of a very useful class of 2-6-2T locomotives designed by Churchward and first introduced into service in 1906. They were very successful; a total of 75 were built in the first two decades of the twentieth century but this one has a unique feature as far as preserved locomotives are concerned. It is the only one that was converted for use with autocoaches while still in service. Others exist with this feature, but they were all converted in preservation, after they had been taken out of service.

The most powerful express steam locomotives ever built for the Great Western were the Kings and Didcot has a fine example, *King Edward II*. Tackling the restoration job, when it was rescued from Barry, was a major undertaking – an undertaking on a scale that no amateur organisation had ever attempted before. It was quite clear that she would never move on a main line again unless supplied with new wheels. Finding a set of wheels for a King that were in good condition proved virtually impossible, so if the locomotive was ever to run there was only one solution; wheels would have to be made. Manufacturing wheels involves two main processes – casting and machining. In order to cast an object in metal, you first need a pattern, traditionally made out of wood. This pattern is packed round with special casting sand and then the pattern is carefully removed, leaving behind a hole of precisely the same shape that can then be filled with molten metal. Some original patterns do exist, but if not, then the only option is to return to the original engineering drawings to find the exact dimensions. These can then go to a professional pattern maker. It is a daunting task for a Society to undertake, but they achieved their goal – though at great expense. It proved to others that it could be done – and some of the most spectacular recreations of recent times such as the Tornado project would have been impossible if they had not followed the GWS lead. Over the years, the Society has had many different parts recast for a number of different projects. The other main task was the first major boiler restoration programme in preservation. The effort was well worth the trouble – even if the whole project took twenty years to complete. But this is the Didcot philosophy; time is never the determining factor. What is essential is that a job is thoroughly done to ensure the preservation of the Great Western legacy into the foreseeable future. It is fair to say that the success of the King restoration process gave the Society the confidence to undertake major projects that would once have been thought impossible.

No 3822 is a heavy freight 2-8-0, one of a class first introduced as far back as 1903 but modified by Collett in 1938. The changes were not very great but did include the addition of side windows to the cab. Some of the class were converted to oil firing during the coal shortage of 1946 but were all converted back again to coal firing. The locomotives of this class were the workhorses of the system and did away with such fripperies as brass-topped chimneys. The class may lack the superficial glamour of the passenger expresses, but 3822 can at least boast rock star status; the locomotive appeared in a Queen video. And for some of the Didcot volunteers, this and the other freight engines in the collection have a special appeal and they have formed their own freight group to care for them. The fact that these locomotives remained in service for so long is a mark of how much they

3650 on the turntable on a Didcot open day.

were valued by the Great Western. At nationalisation, the newly formed Western Division engineers were keen to continue making them but British Rail had a different idea. They were designing an even more powerful class of 2-10-0s, for fast, long distance freight traffic, the 9Fs. The most famous example of that class is, of course, the last steam locomotive ever to be built at Swindon, *Evening Star.*

As mentioned earlier, the decline in traffic from the South Wales coalfield caused some serious rethinking at Swindon. The 42xx class of 2-8-0 tank engines were powerful, but not adapted for long distance travel. Collett decided to modify them by extending the frame, so that a larger coal bunker could be added, and this required an extra pair of trailing wheels, turning the locomotives into a 2-8-2 formation. With a long wheel base and 8-coupled, the engine is fitted with semi-hemispherical rear bearings, acting a bit like ball joints, to make cornering easier.

It had been decided to show the engine as it would have been during service in the Second World War. The side windows are blacked out and in service at night there was a canvas cover. When she was steaming at Didcot, the crew decided to run with the covers on, but found it unbearably hot, so they cheated slightly – they only put the covers on the side that could be seen by the general public. The crews who did actually work during the war years didn't have their option. They are really among the unsung heroes of the war, often working far longer shifts than would normally be permitted by regulations and under the most difficult conditions. The government didn't even make allowance for the hard work they had to endure; they were not eligible for supplementary rations. It is a good thing that their efforts were at least recognised many years later by the volunteers at Didcot.

No 1338 is another of the locomotives not built in Swindon – nor indeed was it originally built for the Great Western. It was constructed by Kitson of Leeds for the Cardiff Railway, a private line owned by the great coal mine and dock owner, the Marquis of Bute. It came into GWR ownership when the line was taken over. In some ways, it looks like a standard small saddle tank, until you notice the valve gear. Instead of being tucked away discreetly, it is in sight above the running board, and it is a most curious thing to see in motion. It is an adaptation of the well-known Walschaert's gear, though that is certainly not immediately apparent. There is a floating lever, attached at one end to the valve spindle and at the

other to the crosshead, and pinned at an intermediate point, not the half way but nearer the spindle and attached to the radius link, so that when everything gets into motion, there is a curious rocking movement, which has been described as looking rather like a spider going for a stroll. This is one of the useful engines for running at Didcot – you can't use the big, impressive Castles and Kings on the short run here. The other late nineteenth century saddle tank from the docks, *Trojan*, was currently away for overhaul. The locomotive was bought by John True in the 1960s from a Tamworth paper mill, where she had been working after being pensioned off by the GWR.

Although the emphasis is inevitably on the steam locomotive, as steam dominated the rail system throughout the history of the GWR, it does not represent the whole story; it was not the only power system in use. Rudolf Diesel had taken out a patent in Britain in the late nineteenth century for an internal combustion engine in which the heat generated by compressing air was used to ignite oil pumped into the combustion chamber. It was an immediate success on road vehicles but its use on the railways proved rather more problematic. The advantages of the system were obvious. Oil had been used instead of coal to raise steam and had proved effective. But used in an internal combustion engine you got six times as

3822 was restored by Didcot's Heavy Freight Group: built in 1940 the locomotive is seen in wartime livery.

The 2-6-2 tank engine is dwarfed by the diesel roommates; in the early days, British Rail still used Didcot.

much power from the same amount of fuel. The difficulty lay in using the power in a locomotive hauling a long train. In the trucks on the road, there was no problem using a clutch and gears, but that was scarcely possible in a main line locomotive. The answer was to use the diesel engine in small units, in other words as rail cars. These were capable of high speeds; the most famous example was built in Germany to run between Berlin and Hamburg which achieved running speeds of approximately 80mph. Its name was *Fliegender Hamburger* that sounds rather comical in translation– the *Flying Hamburger*.

The GWR railcars were very distinctive and one can guess from their styling that the design had its origins in the 1930s, though the Didcot example was built in 1940. There are driving cabs at each end and power is provided by two 9.6 litre, six-cylinder engines. Surprisingly, the engines are remarkably similar to those used on the old red double-decker buses that were such a familiar site on London streets for many years. The railcar idea was developed later into the Diesel Multiple Units that are still in use in the area, though not perhaps as stylish as their predecessor of 1940. The other three diesels on site are there as much for their usefulness as for their historic interest, dating from the '40s and '50s. They are the workhorses of the site and of immense value. One of the great advantages that diesels have over steam locomotives when it comes to the everyday tasks of shunting stock around the site is that they are almost instantly ready for use. No need to get up early to light a fire and stoke a boiler. They are not the most beautiful machines, perhaps summed up by the name of No 26 – 'the Rat'. There is one

Vintage train
days call for vintage costumes – and a little saucy fun.

other interesting example of a non-steam locomotive, No 18000 – a gas turbine. In theory, there are many advantages to using a turbine instead of a piston engine but in practice the prototype was not a success. It was ordered from the Swiss company Brown Boveri in 1946 but when it finally reached Swindon four years later, it was BR who would be testing it out. Gas turbines never really became popular but in America they were adapted from mechanical drive to powering a generator for electric motors and were widely used, especially on big freight trains. The Didcot engine looks well enough from the outside but its working parts were long since removed. A photograph of the original cab shows, rather mysteriously, what appears to be a steering wheel. Needless to say, no one appears to be planning for a full restoration.

The locomotives collection is mostly on show to the general public, but there are always some undergoing repairs or refits in the lifting shop. For safety reasons, this is only accessible to those who work at Didcot or by special invitation. The lifting shed was built here in the 1930s, only partly because of its usefulness. Its construction provided work for the unemployed during the great depression of those years. It was valuable, but major repairs were still carried out Swindon. The main feature is the lifting crane itself, which enables boilers to be removed from the frames, and

The handsome diesel rail car, built in 1940 to a 1930s design.

is invaluable. The shed has some interesting perforations in the fabric, not provided for ventilation, but the result of being hit by shrapnel in Didcot's only air raid. It is odd that the important rail depot was not targeted more often but one theory is that Hitler planned to make Oxford his capital once he had conquered Britain and would have needed it for his own use. But it is only a theory.

The actual locomotive workshop is a comparative newcomer, having been built by the Society in 1988 and fitted out with a variety of machine tools from different sources. Some of them have interesting histories. The oldest is one of the few that actually came from Swindon; manufactured in the 1890s, it was, and still is, used for cutting crosshead bearings using the original jig. The Archdale drill dates back to the First World War and the manufacturers added a plaque to tell future users that it was a wartime product, and not produced with the fine finish that otherwise would have been applied. One of the lathes is associated with one of the great names of twentieth century British engineering – it came from Power Jets, the company started by Sir Frank Whittle, the jet engine pioneer.

For those who do get the chance to visit these areas, there are a lot of fascinating things to see. When an engine has been stripped down, not only do you see parts, such as the boiler, that are normally hidden from view, but you can also see much of the history of the engine and the work that has been carried out, not just in restoration, but earlier at Swindon. One locomotive which was being worked on was the oldest GWR built engine in the collection, the 0-6-0ST No 1363. It may have been built in Swindon, but it certainly is not a typical Great Western locomotive. It has its origins in the Cornwall Mineral Railway. The line had a chequered history, having started life as a horse-worked tramway, later converted to steam. It was built to link the tin and copper mines to ports, but with the slump in the mineral industry, it went into decline, before being acquired by the Great Western at the end of the nineteenth century. During operations, it had been worked by sturdy tank engines, but by the time they arrived at Swindon, they were virtually unworkable, so Churchward handed over the original drawings with the simple instruction – build some new ones like these. This engine was one of them and it has 'foreign' features such as the Allan valve gear, first designed in 1855.

Seeing the work in progress it is sometimes difficult to remember that this is not a professional locomotive workshop, but one

Sometimes when a locomotive had to be moved and no mechanical help was available, the only solution was manpower. Society members and friends hauling *King George V* out of a shed at Swindon.

manned by volunteers. One of the tenders had been flush riveted, a difficult job, but the result shows the skill with which it was carried out. The actual riveting is all but invisible unless you stand right next to the side and look along it to see the fine traces. A problem faced by many restoration societies is recruiting young members, who can be trained to do work of this calibre. Drew Fermore, as a teacher, brought one of his pupils down for work experience. The boy was so impressed that he has been here ever since and is now an adult and an important member of the team. It is good to know that traditions and work practices are being passed on – without them Didcot would eventually be limited to static exhibits, slowly deteriorating and eventually being little better than scrap metal. At any one time, a wide variety of jobs may be going on involving different skills and different engines. To give the reader an idea of the complexity and variety of the work undertaken, I have selected just one of several reports from the locomotive department. This is from the Newsletter of October 1980:

'The axleboxes from the driving axle of 1466 have returned from BREL Swindon following re-metalling of the journal and thrust faces. The horn faces were then re-metalled by ourselves and machined on the refurbished planer. Following the welding of the 14's frames the drag box and most of the other strengthening plates and brackets have been riveted back in place. This enabled the rear of the engine to be lifted so the driving and trailing axles could be put back in their rightful place. New bearings have been fitted to the trailing axle, these being the same as those fitted to standard Great Western tenders. By convenience we had a number of tender bearings re-metalled at Swindon earlier this year. The valve spindle guide liners were also badly worn so these were removed from their housing and re-metalled and machined. The valve spindles were also worn oval and tapered; these have received attention to revert them to being round and parallel again. This work on the valve spindles has been carried out by some of the newer recruits to the locomotives restoration department from the East Midland Group.

'Work continues doing miscellaneous jobs on the frames of 3822 whilst waiting for the wheels to be returned from the Severn Valley Railway. Work has started on re-bushing the brakegear and while the boiler is off the frames the opportunity was taken to remove the cast iron front sandbox from between the frames. At the same time the rear of the cylinder block was cleaned down and re-lagged. The sandbox was soon cleaned down and painted but re-fitting proved to be a problem. On the first attempt the job had to be carried on into the hours of darkness one Saturday evening before the box was secure and the diesel crane released from its long ordeal. Still a second attempt had to be made as there was one single bolt head on the lagging fouling the sandbox and lining up with its bolt holes on the main frames.'

Mentioning scrap metal, it is also perhaps as well to remember that there is one other organisation without whom the whole restoration

An impressive array of Society and visiting locomotives: they are from left to right, the first 100mph locomotive *City of Truro*; *Drysllwyn Castle*; Jubilee Class 45596; and *Duke of Gloucester*.

programme, not just here but on preserved lines throughout the country, would be very different. Woodham Brothers of Barry Island accepted 297 steam engines from British Rail for cutting up – but over 200 of them never saw the cutter's torch. They were bought for preservation and if they had not been saved at Barry, half the current Didcot collection would not exist. Dai Woodham is being remembered at Didcot. A County Class is currently under construction and is to be named *County of Glamorgan* in his honour.

Recording the fact that a locomotive was acquired from Barry is only the start of the story; it then had to be moved to Didcot. No 5051 *Earl Bathurst* made the journey in February 1970, together with a brake van and a tender for No 7808, hauled by Hymek diesel 7052. A speed limit of 25mph was imposed and inspection stops were planned every 25 miles. The little procession left Barry at 9.10 in the morning and as inspections showed no hint of trouble, the process was speeded up and it arrived at Gloucester 20 minutes early; that time was soon lost as it was reported that a line side detector had reported a hot box, but inspection of both engines showed no sign of trouble. They were allowed to proceeded through a wintry landscape, past the attractive Golden Valley en route to Swindon.

It was decided to make a show of arriving back at the locomotive's birthplace, so a number of oily rags were set fire to and placed in the firebox, producing a convincing stream of smoke from the chimney. In spite of the delays, they reached Didcot 5 minutes ahead of schedule. It was a long, hard day in bad conditions, but there was now another classic locomotive to add to the growing collection.

APPENDIX: LOCOMOTIVES

This section gives more detail on locomotives not discussed in the main part of this chapter. Locomotives will have been built at Swindon for the GWR unless otherwise specified.

1, 0-4-0ST *Bonnie Prince Charlie*, built at RSH in 1949, worked mainly at Poole Harbour

5, 0-4-0WT *Shannon/Jane. Shannon* was the original name. Worked at various tasks including a short stay at the Cromford & High Peak and then as a shunter at Crewe before going to Wantage. Built in 1857 by George England and worked originally on the Sandy and Potten Railway

1014, 4-6-0 *County of Glamorgan.* At the time of writing, the locomotive is under construction by the GWS at Didcot. This is a rebuild that is described in more detail in Chapter 5.

1338, 0-4-0ST. Built by Kitson & Co in 1898 and worked originally on the Cardiff Dock Railway

1340 0-4-0ST *Trojan.* The locomotive had to be fitted with a substitute boiler at Didcot, built in 1897 by Avonside Engine Co. of Bristol. First ran on the Alexandra Dock Railway which was then taken over by the GWR, after which it was moved around the system. When acquired, it needed a new boiler, and eventually went into steam in 2002. Currently on static display.

1363 0-6-0ST. 1361 Class. Ran for a time on public roads at Weymouth, where it was fitted with a warning bell in front of the cab. Built 1910

1466/4866 48xx/14xx Class. Originally numbered 4866 and renumbered 1466 in 1946. Built 1936, the class was originally designed for push-pull working.

2409 0-6-0 *King George.* Built by Hunslet, Leeds in 1942. First worked at Linby Colliery. In spite of its name, it has very little in common with the main line express Kings.

2999 4-6-0 *Lady of Legend.* A Star class locomotive currently under construction by the GWS at Didcot.

3650 0-6-0PT. This and 3738 belong to the 57xx Class that developed out of the 27xx shunters introduced in 1901. Improvements in boiler design resulted in the class being changed from saddle tanks to pannier tanks. Built in 1939.

3738 0-6-0PT. Built 1937.

3822 2-8-0 2884 Class; the locomotive is currently on static display and will need a complete boiler overhaul before going back into service. Built 1940.

4079 4-6-0 *Pendennis Castle*. Built 1924.

4144 2-6-2T 41xx Class. Built 1946.

4709 2-8-0 47xx Class. These massive engines were designed by Churchward and intended for use in mixed traffic, but mainly worked heavy night freights, earning them the nickname 'Night Owls'. None of the class has survived, but one is being built at Llangollen for the GWS.

5051 4-6-0 *Drysllwyn Castle/Earl Bathurst*. Built 1936.

5227 2-8-0T 5205 Class. Used as a source of parts in the construction of No 4709. Built 1924.

5322 2-6-0 43xx Class. Built 1917.

5572 2-6-2T 4575 Class. The 45xx was developed from the 44xx with larger driving wheels for extra speed. The subclass was introduced in February 1927 with larger tanks and a heavier overall weight. Built 1927.

5900 4-6-0 *Hinderton Hall*. Rescued from Barry by a Society member and brought to Didcot in 1970 and fully restored, but now in the queue for an overhaul. Built 1931.

6023 4-6-0 *King Edward II*. The Kings were developed by Collett from the Castle class and were the most powerful locomotives ever built for the GWR. Kings were capable of covering the 117½ miles from Bristol to Paddington in 100 minutes. The fastest service available in 2017 is 97 minutes. Built 1930.

6106 2-6-2T 61xx Class. This class derived from the 51xx, itself based on an earlier Churchward design. The locomotives were mainly intended for London suburban services, but 6106 had a moment in the limelight, appearing dressed in psychedelic colours in the movie *The Bliss of Mrs. Blossom*. Built in 1931.

6697 0-6-2T 56xx Class. Built at Armstrong Whitworth in 1928.

6998 4-6-0 *Burton Agnes Hall*. On static exhibition, awaiting overhaul; built 1949.

7202 2-8-2T 72xx Class. Being restored. Built 1934.

7808 4-6-0 *Cookham Manor*. A very successful class and the engine was not bought from scrap but directly from BR when it came out of service. Built 1938.

Firefly 2-2-2. The replica of one of Gooch's Firefly Class, completed at Didcot in 2005 by the Firefly Trust.

Iron Duke 4-2-2. The other replica of a Gooch locomotive at Didcot. Built by RESCO in 1985 for the National Railway Museum.

93 Steam railmotor, originally built 1908 and rebuilt at Didcot.

22 Diesel railcar, built in 1940. There are only three of these vehicles surviving and this is the only one in operational condition.

DL26 0-6-0. Built by Hunslet in 1957 and named 'The Rat'.

08604 0-6-0 Diesel Electric *Phantom*, built at BR Derby works in 1959.

D9516 0-6-0. A diesel locomotive with hydraulic transmission, a class popularly known as 'Teddy Bear', built in 1964 at BR Swindon.

18000 A1A-A1A *Kerosene Castle*. A prototype gas turbine locomotive built in 1949 by Brown Boveri, Switzerland, and operated by BR.

CHAPTER FOUR

Carriages and Wagons

Rolling stock often appears to the outsider to be the Cinderella of the preservation movement, not having the glamour and excitement of the steam locomotives. Yet without the rolling stock, locomotives are meaningless; their sole purpose is to move freight and people from one place to another. And once one starts looking into the history of carriages and wagons, they can seem every bit as fascinating as their puffing companions. Carriages in particular have an intriguing story to tell of social life in Britain and the changes it has seen since those first passengers took a journey behind a steam locomotive over Great Western rails. The Centre holds a great variety of coaches, ranging all the way from replicas of the original broad gauge coaches to the most exotic rolling stock.

In the early days, first class passengers travelled in a certain degree of comfort in six-wheeled coaches, looking rather as if four old-fashioned stage coaches had been rammed together. But they had proper covering, glazed windows and plush, well upholstered seating. The replica second and third class coaches show a great contrast. The second class is rough and ready, but at least has built up sides and a roof – but no glass in the windows. The third is simply an open wagon with crude benches. These third class 'coaches' were often overcrowded but no one seemed unduly worried until Christmas Eve 1842, when two of these thirds were attached to the 4.30 a.m. goods train from Paddington to Bristol. There had been heavy rain that night that had resulted in a landfall in the deep cutting at Sonning. The locomotive ploughed straight into it and as the train was loose coupled, the first of the passenger third coaches was crushed against the tender. Eight passengers were killed and seventeen were seriously injured. Even a tragedy on this scale might not have excited much attention among the powers that be but most of the men had been working on building the new House of Commons and were on their way home for the holiday. As a result, the politicians took an interest and there was an official enquiry that resulted in the Act of 1844, promoted by William Gladstone. This specified that all railway companies had to provide at least one train a day, in each direction, running at a speed

The Dreadnought coach was one of the first to be acquired by the Society and is seen being fitted with new panels.

of no less than 12 miles per hour, and that it should contain covered carriages with seats for third class passengers, at the rate of no more than a penny a mile. They came to be known as 'Parliamentary trains' and marked the start of improved conditions for all classes of passengers. Nothing else in the collection has the crudity and discomfort of these broad gauge coaches.

At the very opposite end of the scale are the luxury coaches, the super saloons or 'Ocean coaches'. Eight of these were built to provide a service between Paddington and Plymouth for passengers on the transatlantic liners. Most of these travelled between France and America, calling into the English port along the way. Each of these coaches was given a suitably aristocratic name and the third in the series, No 9113 built in 1937, was the *Prince of Wales*. This was one of three saved by the GWS, all of which finished up at Didcot, but not by a direct route. 9113 had been privately bought and spent a certain amount of time on the Severn Valley Railway. But it had endured a hard life since taken out of full-time service and at first after it had been bequeathed to the Great Western Society, it languished in the stock shed. Nothing much happened to it in the 1970s and '80s but a certain amount of restoration work got under way in 1991. But like all such projects, a long view has to be taken, and work done as and when funds become available. It is a sad fact of life in the carriage department, that it is a great deal easier to raise cash for locomotive restoration than it is for coaches. Nevertheless, when this chapter was being written, restoration on 9113 was all but complete. The story of the restoration gives a good example of why carriage restoration is not necessarily any easier or cheaper than locomotive restoration.

When work started on the coach, the first essential was to find out exactly what had been done and what still needed to be done. When the coaches were built, the metal panels were flush but they had become buckled and although an attempt had been made at some time to weld everything back together, it had clearly not worked. The decision was taken to strip off all the panels and remove the glass. Once the latter had been taken out, it was a legal requirement that it could not be put back but had to be replaced by modern safety glass. With the panels removed, it was possible to assess the state of the wooden frame; some sections were sound, others needed remedial work and a large amount of timber had to be replaced. An outside contractor, Mark Werrell, was brought in to do some work but it was obvious that a complete restoration was going to be costly and would require a major fundraising exercise.

One of the Society's vintage coaches: the Dean 4-wheel brake 3rd class was built in 1891 and spent some years as a GWR Camp Coach.

Work temporarily came to a halt but it provided an opportunity to work on another luxury vehicle with an intriguing history.

Coach No 9002 'a Collett Special Saloon' is another of the luxury coaches, described as a VIP coach and built in 1940. According to tradition, it was used by General Eisenhower when he was in Britain in charge of the D-Day operations. There is no documentary evidence to support this, but there are some physical features to suggest it could well be true. The roof had been reinforced and the panelling electrically earthed but most significantly, it was fitted with a substantial radio aerial, which would obviously have been essential for wartime communications. After the war, it was used as a GWR royal coach for a time. It was given a major refit at Swindon in the 1950s, and the two saloons were refurbished with splendid Tiger's Eye English walnut panelling; while the dining table and suspended light fittings were given a burr walnut veneer – the veneer on the lights also needed a certain amount of restoration. The seating was reupholstered and the coach is today fully restored to its former glory.

Once that work was completed and the coffers replenished, it was time to return to the *Prince of Wales*. Mark Werrell, who had already done some of the work, was now taken on as a full-time carpenter and is still hard at work at Didcot. There was a great deal that still needed to be done. All the walnut window mouldings, for example, had to be renovated. But that was a comparatively simple job; Mick Howse, who is in charge of the coach and wagon section, took them home and did the work in his garage. The biggest problem was the internal panelling. It all looked very fine, but although the main framework is solid walnut, the panels themselves are simply plywood that had been stained to look like walnut. Unfortunately, woodworm had got into most of those panels, which would have to be replaced. There was, however, one piece of good news; the curved panels that would have been very difficult to reproduce were unaffected and the actual framework was sound. There was a problem in getting the right walnut effect. Originally, spirit-based dyes would have been used, but nowadays most dyes are water-based and are not so good for this purpose. The first attempts came out quite orange, but a supplier was found who could provide the spirit variety, which solved the problem.

Wood in the coaches was French polished – not a skill that anyone in the Society had then acquired, so a certain amount of trial and error was involved. The old craftsmen would have applied as many

A 1930 passenger brake van stripped down to its frame for restoration.

as twenty or thirty coats to get that deep shine of the best furniture, but the polish is soft and easily damaged. It was decided that it made sense to apply a clear varnish over the top as a protection. This resulted in a certain amount of tut-tutting among the purists, who wanted everything done just as it had been originally back at Swindon. Then someone unearthed an old GWR magazine that described how the company had faced the same problem and come up with exactly the same solution – they too had over-varnished. Today, the panelling looks fine, apart from the gaps that have been left to take photographs. The original photographs still exist of Plymouth, Marazion and various West Country resorts, and each gap has been labelled so that each photo will be placed just as it was half a century and more ago.

The inside of the carriage is what most impresses the visitors and very fine it looks too, with a private end compartment for four passengers and a larger saloon. The toilets contained 'modern' melamine lavatories, which have now been removed and the old toilet compartments are now used to store folding tables and have been repainted in traditional colours. What the visitor will be less aware of is the work that has been done elsewhere. The roof has been taken off in sections and renovated. The ceilings have all been down and the whole coach rewired to provide power to such essentials for any luxury coach as the buttons by the seats that would be pressed to summon an attendant. Originally, there was a full set of table lamps but by the time the coach reached Didcot, only one had survived – somewhere scattered around Britain there are homes lit by historic GWR lamps. New ones will have to be made to match the lone survivor. On the engineering side, the bogies have been removed and stripped right down to their basic components and thoroughly checked. The brakes have been overhauled, the cylinders and direct action valves checked. At the time of writing, there was a certain amount of rodding to complete, but this is a comparatively minor job.

There is one very obvious difference between the ocean coaches and even the most luxurious first class coaches in use on other trains. Instead of fixed seating, they were fitted out with padded armchairs and sofas so that passengers were, in effect, enjoying the comforts of a well-furnished home – but one that moved. The coaches were originally fitted out by a company called Trollope, but later by the GWR themselves so there are variations between the upholstery styles in different sections. The Trollope originals had an ornate pattern, showing a rural scene with rivers and trees; the GWR seats were upholstered in powder blue. The furniture was re-covered in the 1950s and re-covering now would be prohibitively expensive – about £3-400 per unit, and there are 50 or so seats in the coach. When the coach enters service at Didcot, it will probably be fitted out with seats taken from the other preserved special saloons,

Restoring internal panels of the *Prince of Wales* coach.

where reupholstering had already been carried out. Research has shown that the tables were covered with dark brown cloth and there was a matching carpet. Curtains, however, were altogether more ornate in gold and silver damask. Rather more modest, but appropriate, materials will be used in the refit.

Six of the eight Ocean coaches were similar to this one. In their original state, however, passengers expected a full meal service in these carriages, but that could only be supplied by adding on a whole restaurant car. This was a waste of resources when only the kitchen section would actually be needed. So the decision was taken to change the last two of the set by including kitchens. 'Princess Elizabeth' was one of those coaches, in which the small private compartment and one of the lavatories was removed to make way for the kitchen in 1937. The three Ocean saloons at Didcot all needed extensive work – far from completed on the other two – though the good news was that wheels and tyres did not show much sign of wear. On other sets in the collection, the quote for fixing and retyring was £30,000. So at least on the heavy engineering side, things looked good. One broken spring was discovered which came as an unpleasant surprise, this is not something one would normally expect to find. It was sent away and returned with certification that it was now fit for use.

Years of work and a great deal of money have been expended on restoring the Prince of Wales coach, but the end result is a vehicle that will offer Didcot's visitors what must be the most luxurious ride available on any railway in Britain. Just as importantly, for

Reupholstering a compartment in a Collett 'Sunshine' coach from the 1940s.

all those involved, the work has been done as far as possible in a way that is faithful to the original design, preserving memories of days when Brunel's great original dream was realised – steam locomotives would take passengers from London and deliver them to a port from which steam powered ships would carry them across the Atlantic. It is just a shame that the port of embarkation was not, as Brunel would have wished, Bristol.

Every coach in the collection has a different story to tell and the story that is made apparent will be different at any particular time, depending on the state of restoration. There are three carriages in the collection that date back to the period from 1877 to 1902 when William Dean was superintendent of locomotive, carriage and wagon design. One of these, No 290, is a 6-wheel coach with 1st, 2nd and 3rd class compartments squeezed into a comparatively small body. It was in the worst condition of any coach that had ever arrived on site and requires substantial rebuild – which will have to include providing new doors and completely remaking the interior. Stripped back to the frame, one can at least admire the work of the carpenters and joiners, craftsmanship of a very high order; that craftsmanship is being matched by the workers of today. Looking at Victorian coaches that are not fully restored reveals all sorts of fascinating details. Floor planks for example were laid in a chevron pattern in two layers, so that the diagonals of the top layer ran in the opposite direction from those underneath, ensuring great strength and stability. Interior design also reflects the different periods in which coaches were built, varying from the rather ornate work of the Victorian and Edwardian age to the angular Art Deco of the 1930s. The restorers work hard to ensure that these essential differences are preserved. One also becomes aware that travel in Victorian coaches could be quite a tricky business. Another Dean coach is No 1941 that from the outside looks quite modern, apart from the clerestory windows at the top providing extra light. There were gas tanks under the frame for lighting at night. This was a third class carriage with eight compartments – but no corridor. What did a passenger do if caught short on a long journey? That is probably a question it is best not to explore. The finest example of a coach from the 1930s is No 1289, built in 1937. The interior is very stylish, with light birch panelling inlaid with mahogany. The furnishings are in a typical Thirties fashion, perhaps seen most strikingly in the mirrors engraved with the GWR monogram. This uses a pure art deco typeface.

The sumptuous interior of the Collett Special Saloon, designed specifically for VIPs.

There are too many coaches to describe all of them and their restoration in detail, but one class does deserve a special mention, as it was an important and integral part of trains for much of the railway's history – the brake van. Generally, this would be incorporated into a passenger carriage as a separate compartment. The name derives from the presence of a screw brake, but the compartment was often referred to as either the guard's van or the luggage van. Both terms were reasonable as the compartment did indeed always provide a space for the guard and often contained luggage. The van was often used to carry mail bags or to deliver daily papers from London to towns around the country and it was certainly not unknown for more exotic objects to be carried. The author, when spending a vacation working as a porter, remembers loading racing pigeons, which received more tender care than most commonplace luggage. There are several examples and there is also a bow-ended full brake from the 1930s that is being fitted out to accompany the travelling post office that is described below. But not all the coaches are included in the historic collection. Several from the British Rail era perform useful functions on the site. A pair from 1969 house the Science, Learning and Railways facility;

a 1960 coach is now the Black Python Bar and a 1962 coach is used as a support vehicle for rail tours. The other BR coach is a sleeper, now used as an occasional dormitory.

One vehicle attracts more visitor interest than any other, especially when seen in action – the travelling post office. What makes this special is the way in which it could be used to collect and drop off mail bags without having to stop the train. For collection, mail bags were suspended from poles, and using a lever inside the van, a net was swung out from the side to scoop up the bag. Delivery was simpler; the bag was attached to an arm swung out to the side and a catch released it to drop at the trackside. On the inside of the coach, the mail could be sorted, dropped into pigeon holes, according to their destination – an operation famously captured in the film *Night Mail*, with W. H. Auden's poem, working to the rhythm of the train as commentary. Didcot is one of the very few places where one can still see this system being demonstrated.

Different coaches present different problems and the work area where restoration is carried out has been designed in a logical fashion. There are two stagings in the coach bay, one to provide low level access, the other to allow work on the roof. The coach that was being worked on was next to the higher level and that allowed one to see just how thoughtful the engineers of the early twentieth century were in thinking about what might go wrong and how to minimise the damage. The roof consists of plates of 16-gauge steel that reach down over the sides of the coach, where they are screwed on and the gutters screwed through. Damage can occur if water isn't cleared from the gutters when it can seep through into the ceilings. To make repairs, it is not necessary to remove the whole roof to reach the gutter plates. The bottom ten inches can be ground away so that the main roof needn't be touched, and this sacrificial piece can be replaced and riveted back on. The work force can manage pop riveting, but not large-scale hot riveting.

The staging is also used for painting, though small painting jobs are carried out in a separate workshop in a former coach. Painting is not just a case of getting the colours right and applying numerous layers to get the typical gloss of a well-maintained coach. It is often necessary to provide lining and lettering and, in some cases, quite complex monograms and emblems. This calls for a specialist. At Didcot, the job has gone to a painter who started out painting survivors from the predecessors of the railway age – canal narrow boats. What they have in common is the need to maintain traditional details, but in the case of canal boats, there is much more freedom in providing the typical 'roses and castles' decoration and ornate lettering. He did not, however, have any specialist knowledge of the railways. So at Didcot, the painter was supplied with the appropriate designs, which he was able to copy with complete accuracy. That is one part of the restoration programme that requires outside help to be brought in. But a large amount of the work is done by Mick Howse, Mark Werrell and their team of volunteers in the carpentry workshop.

In order to carry out a wide range of activities at Didcot, it is not only necessary to have appropriate machinery, but also buildings

Right and opposite:
Hanging mail bags on the gantry, from which they will be picked up by the Post Office van, which has a net to collect the bags, without the train having to stop.

in which to house them – and these were not always available when the Society first moved in. One essential for all carpentry is a supply of properly seasoned timber – and that requires timber stores. Didcot now has two, one for coaches and the other for wagons; the timber for the latter can be far rougher than that used on sophisticated coaches. The stores are not only fit for purpose but are also based on original GWR designs – in this case, a timber store at Taunton. When new timber is first brought in, it has to be dried in a kiln and then brought to the store to be seasoned. The buildings have slatted sides to allow the free circulation of air but keep out the light. The timbers are regularly turned to ensure they season evenly and after about six months can be brought straight into the workshop and are ready for use.

The workshop has most of the machines you would expect; lathes, drills and saws, many acquired second hand – one vintage drill came from the famous Brakspear Brewery at Henley. There is a mortise machine to help in making mortis and tenon joints and a plane that can be worked to extremely fine tolerances. The most advanced machine is the super moulder for creating intricate patterns that only Mark is qualified to use. Pattern making is an important part of the work. It is often necessary to cast replacements for different parts and before they can be produced in metal, a wooden pattern has to be made. The more work is done, the greater the number of jigs that become available. Modern technology has come into play. For example, steel and oak are not happy companions as the acid in the wood tends to attack the steel, leading to splits. There are two ways to overcome this; either use stainless steel or use a different wood. Sapele, also known as African mahogany, does not react with steel and is now generally used. Some innovations, however, are definitely frowned on. The Phillips screw, so beloved of DIYers, is never used; the screw may be easier to put in, but it is a devil to get out. On the engineering side, it is often necessary to jack up coaches to take out the bogies for a thorough investigation and overhaul. Fortunately, bogies are interchangeable for most of the coaches – but not for the early examples from the Dean era. Replacing any of those would be extremely difficult and very expensive.

So far, there has been no mention of wagons and other rolling stock. One can see why many visitors tend to pass them by with only a brief glance; they are never likely to go for a ride in them. Yet it is worth remembering that steam railways came into existence in the first place to move freight, not people. Even the famous Stockton & Darlington Railway only used locomotives for freight; passengers were carried in a horse drawn stage coach that only differed from the counterpart on the roads by having flanged wheels adapted to run on rails. Wagons in fact can be fascinating, because so many

Volunteers at work riveting the frame of a slate wagon.

are special adaptations designed for a specific commodity. And if, as the GWS have always intended, you want to present a picture of all the railway's activities, the wagons must have a place of honour.

Once you start actually looking at wagons in detail, you begin to realise what a great variety there are. Even such commonplace vehicles as open trucks and vans have their own variations. Some of them even have quite exotic histories and none more so than wagon No 41934. To give it its full title, this is a 'Crocodile F' bogie well wagon, built in 1908. It looks very like the low loaders often seen on our roads today, which is not surprising as it was performing much the same function on the railroad, transporting large and awkward objects such as locomotive boilers. It was sent out with the British Expeditionary Force to France in the Second World War but abandoned after the evacuation of the troops from Dunkirk. It was promptly put to use in the German army and was sent to the Eastern Front. Following D-Day, it was recaptured, this time by the Americans and returned to service with the allies, before demob and return to Britain after the war. It had a long history but was originally destined for an ignominious end; it was sent to Barry scrap yard for breaking up. Fortunately, Society members spotted it, recognised its importance and the Crocodile is now at Didcot.

A good deal of freight was carried in simple open wagons, with little to distinguish them, apart from the fact that some had sides that were three planks high and others were five plank; Didcot has examples of both. But there were also specialised wagons. The oldest in the collection is a bolster wagon built in Swindon in 1881. It was a low wagon that takes its names from the wooden bolsters, timber baulks on which the load was rested and held in place by movable spikes. The next oldest is a tar wagon, built in 1898 by Charles Robert & Co. who had works near Wakefield. In the days before North Sea gas came on line, Britain had a huge number of gasworks, supplying gas initially for lighting and heating, but later merely for heating. The gas was produced by heating coal in retorts and tar was one of the by-products. This was a valuable material used for all kinds of purposes, such as making tarmac for road surfacing. So this messy, sticky and generally unpleasant substance was moved around in large quantities and as no one wanted it spread over other rolling stock, it was carried in closed tanks and tar tanks were generally coupled together to keep them separate from other traffic. They are very distinctive. Cattle

The restored slate wagon with a 'Toad' in the background – the unusual name comes from the GWR telegraph code for a brake van.

wagons, on the other hand, look much like other vans, except that there is a gap between the sides and the roof to provide ventilation. The other important commodity that came from farms and was distributed around the country in literally millions of gallons a day was milk. In the early days, metal churns were loaded into special vans, but later the churns were abandoned for specialist vehicles. The example here has a stainless steel tank to prevent any contamination.

Long after vacuum braking had been introduced on all passenger trains, goods wagons were still loose coupled and individual vehicles were fitted with hand brakes that were only useful when shunting. As a consequence, the brake van with a screw-down brake was an essential feature of goods trains. The common types of goods brake van were known as 'Toads'. The name had nothing to do with any resemblance to croaking animals in ponds but was simply the telegraphic identification then in use for a brake van. The Tadpole, however, was not as you might expect a small brake van but an open fish wagon. The Toad vans consist of a closed compartment with windows at both ends and a covered veranda at one end. Footboards with handrails down the side meant the guard could get a clear view of what was happening during shunting. As well as the screw brake, the van had sand boxes, a set of tools and, for the guard's comfort, a seat and a stove. Even after vacuum braking was fully introduced, the guard's van was an important part of any goods train.

Things go wrong, even on the best run railways, so it was essential that breakdown vehicles were available so that men and the necessary tools could be brought quickly to the scene of the trouble. The Society has two riding vans and two tool vans, all built at Swindon in 1908. And, of course, there are vehicles that are in use still at Didcot for all kinds of work, such as moving rails, sleepers and ballast. Two venerable mobile hand cranes are also available; a 3-ton version built in 1899 and its big brother, a 12-ton crane of 1894. Goods vehicles are as varied as carriages or locomotives and are not only there as exhibits that help to tell the GWR story, but many are also an essential part of the operations on the site.

APPENDIX: CARRIAGES IN THE HISTORIC COLLECTION

The following is a complete list of all the carriages in the historic collection, with brief notes on those not already described in some detail in the main text. The date for each entry is the original date of construction.

92 Churchward auto trailer, 1912.
111 Collett full brake, 1934.
190 Collett auto trailer, 1933. Although this carriage was bought in 1970, it was not restored until 1996. The interior has been restored using reclaimed oak from old church pews and reupholstered using a GWR pattern from 1937.
231 Hawksworth auto trailer, 1951. This was the last version of the auto trailer to be built. It has been reupholstered in the 1949 version of blue.
250 Broad gauge body, nineteenth century. Not exactly a full body – only the end section is on display.
290 Dean 4-wheel composite, 1902. This carriage had had a somewhat chequered career. When a film company was looking for a 4-wheel coach, the original body was replaced by a period replica. This was later removed and the original is being

restored. An unusual feature of this carriage is the use of Mansell wheels. These were designed and patented by William Mansell of the South Eastern Railway as composite wooden wheels with a solid centre. They were constructed out of hardwearing teak and were used because they made less noise than conventional iron or steel wheels.

316 Hawksworth full brake, 1950. This was acquired from the Nene Valley Railway, where it was used as a shop and now has slipped further down the social scale and is a humble locker room.

333 Hawksworth full brake, 1951. The carriage is now used as a shop space for the Antiquary and Oxford Group.

416 Dean 4-wheel brake third, 1891. This was first converted in GWR days into a camper van and there are still bunk beds in the guard's van.

484 Churchward 'Monster' covered carriage truck, 1913.

536 Collett 8-compartment 'Sunshine' third, 1940. A corridor coach, it was on loan to the South Devon Railway, who restored it as part of the loan agreement, including complete reupholstering.

565 Churchward 'Python' covered carriage truck, 1914. Now used as a workshop and store.

814 Travelling post office, 1940.

861 Replica 6-wheeled third constructed for the National Railway Museum, 1984.

862 Replica 6-wheeled second, also built for the NRM, 1984.

933 Dean full brake, 1898. The Victorians were apt to travel with large luggage items, such as trunks, that could not fit into passenger compartments. Special luggage vans such as this, with two compartments and a vestibule for the guard, were introduced to take luggage and parcels.

975 Dean 4-wheel third, 1902. Scheduled for restoration.

1111 Collett 8-compartment 'Sunshine' third, 1938. Similar to 536.

1159 Medical officer's coach (converted). Originally Churchward passenger brake van toplight, 1925.

1184 Collett bow-ended full brake, 1930. Originally used for luggage, parcels and mail with two compartments either side of the guard's compartment, it is being restored for use with the travelling post office.

1289 Collett 'Excursion' third, 1937.

1357 Dean 8-compartment third clerestory, 1903.

1941 Dean 8-compartment third clerestory, 1901. The coach has eight compartments but no corridor or toilet facilities. The clerestory roof allows for the tall gas lamps to be placed well clear of passengers' heads – the gas was contained in a tank beneath the coach.

2202 Hawksworth 4-compartment brake third, 1950. The carriage is unusual in having been built at Metropolitan Cammell, who remained in business right up to 2005.

2232 Hawksworth 4-compartment third, 1950. Currently being restored as a staff locker room.

2511 Dean third 'family' saloon, 1894. Carriages such as this were available for private hire by families who could afford to pay for exclusivity; the larger versions had separate compartments for servants and a kitchen. This example still has original features, including the upholstery and hand-coloured photographs decorate the walls.

2796 Collett 'Syphon G' bogie milk van, 1937. This dates from the time when milk was moved in churns, now mainly seen as 'period' features on preserved lines.

3299 Churchward 'Dreadnought' 9-compartment third, 1905.

3755 Churchward 'Main Line & City' toplight, 1921. The coach gets regular outings behind Thomas the Tank Engine.

3756 Churchward 'Main Line & City' toplight, 1921. Originally built to serve the suburban lines from Paddington, it was later used as a miners' train on the Glyncornwg line in South Wales.

3963 Churchward toplight corridor third, 1919. Last used as a camping coach.

4553 Collett 8-compartment bow-ended third, 1925. Used for storage.

5085 Collett 8-compartment bow-ended third, 1928.

5787 Collett brake third, 1933.

5952 Collett 8-compartment third, 1935. A coach in good condition but needs reupholstering.

6824 Dean clerestory tri-composite, 1887.Currently undergoing restoration, this coach was originally built for the broad gauge.

7285 Collett 'Sunshine' composite, 1941. The coach has a permanent home beside the tracks.

7313 Collett 'Sunshine' composite, 1940. The coach is being fitted out just as it would have been in wartime, with economy brown, subdued lighting and blackout arrangements.

7371 Collett 'Sunshine' brake composite, 1941. In its latter days in service, it formed part of the Swindon test train. After running for a time at Didcot, it was taken out of service for refurbishment. It was assumed that it would be a simple repaint, but considerable work was needed, during which the windows were replaced with safety glass. The Society has examples of the original fabrics – green sea shell moquette for third class and brown with gold piping moquette for first. A company in Abingdon was able to supply matching fabrics.

7372 Hawksworth brake composite, 1948. One of the last coaches to be built by the GWR and originally part of the royal train. It is interesting in that it has aluminium fittings in first class but conventional brass in third. It still has its original upholstery but is now rather the worse for the wear and will eventually be replaced by new material of the same design. It is in service and is a regular addition to the Thomas train.

7976 Collett Brake composite, 1923.

9002 Collett special saloon, 1940.

9083 Hawksworth first class sleeper, 1951. There are ten compartments, each fitted with connecting doors, a single bed and wash basin. There is a small steward's kitchen and a lavatory. It has almost all its original fittings intact and is jointly owned by eleven GWS volunteer members.

9112 Collett super saloon 'Queen Mary', 1932.

9113 Collett super saloon 'Prince of Wales', 1932.

9118 Collett super saloon 'Princess Elizabeth', 1932.

9520 Dean tri-composite kitchen-diner, 1903. This is the first GWR coach to be fitted with a central kitchen.

9635 Collett 'Centenary' first class kitchen-diner, 1935. The coach was one of a pair built for the Cornish Riviera Limited. The coach is unusually wide at 9ft 7in. The kitchen is almost exactly as it was when built apart from the addition of a ventilation fan and the use of propane instead of oil gas.

APPENDIX: WAGONS IN THE HISTORIC COLLECTION

Where there are no notes beside an entry, that is either because it has already been discussed in the main text or because the title is self-explanatory. Most of the names, such as 'mica', are simply the GWR telegraph code names for that class of wagon and bear little resemblance to what they might be carrying. 'Bloater' is a notable exception.

1 Tar wagon, 1898.
18 Open wagon 5 plank, 1927.
101 6 Wheel drinking water tank wagon, 1948.

263 Signal & Telegraph Department mess van, 1952. It was converted into a mess van by British Rail.

745 Oil tank wagon, 1912.

752 Special cattle van, 1952.

2671 'Bloater' fish van, 1925.

2862 'Fruit C' fruit van, 1939.

2913 'Fruit D' fruit van, 1941. The van is similar to 2862, but of rather cruder construction, reflecting wartime austerity.

3030 'Rotank' flat wagon, 1947. The name is an abbreviation of 'road tank', which the wagon carried.

4166 Goods van, 1942. This and 4167 are odd men out, having been built for the London, Midland & Scottish at their Wolverton works.

4167 Goods van, 1942.

10153 Open wagon-7 plank – undated. Began its working life on the Taff Vale.

11152 'Iron mink', 1900. The 'iron' in the name simply indicates that it is iron- bodied not timber.

17447 'Toad A' 20T brake van, 1940.

19818 'Open A' goods wagon, 1917.

32337/8 Twin 'Mites' single bolster wagons, 1881. These are articulated, carried on two sets of 4-wheel bogies.

41723 'Coral A' wagon for crated glass, 1908.

41934 bogie well wagon 'Crocodile F', 1908.

42193 'Hydra D' well wagon, 1917.

42239 Grain wagon, 1927.

42271 'Loriot L' well wagon, 1934.

43949 Cylindrical tank wagon, 1901.

47886 'Fruit' van, 1892.

56400 'Toad', 1900.

63066 Loco coal wagon, 1946.

68684 'Toad', 1924.

70335 'Macaw B', 1939.

79933 'Tevan', 1922.

80659 Ballast wagon, 1936.

80668 Ballast wagon, 1936.

80789 Ballast wagon, 1937.

82917 Pooley workshop van, 1911. Built originally as a standard van, it was converted into a travelling workshop for Henry Pooley & Sons. They were a major manufacturer of weighing machines, later taken over by the well known company W. & T. Avery.

84997/8/9/85000 Articulated wagon 'Pollen E', 1909. Set of four originally designed to carry naval guns; on loan from the National Railway Museum.

92943 China clay wagon (5-plank), 1913.

94835 'Open C' open wagon, 1920.

100377 Shunter's truck, 1953.

100682 Wagon 4 chaired sleepers, 1939.

101720 'Mink A' van, 1924.

101836 'Mink A' van, 1925.

105599 'Fruit B' banana van, 1929.

105742 Motor car van 'Mogo', 1936. This is just what the name suggests – a van designed to take cars.

105781 Gunpowder van; the essential difference between this and similar vans lies in the interior, where everything is designed to avoid any possibility of creating sparks and explosions. The lining is wood, held by brass screws and there are hooks for plain leather boots for the workers, whose normal hob-nailed boots could create the lethal spark. Many were adaptations of Mink vans, such as 112843, 1939.

105860 'Mica B' refrigerated van, 1925.

112843 'Mink G' van, 1931.

116954 Motor car van 'Asmo', 1930.

117993 Open goods wagon, 1931.

143698 Open goods wagon, 1945.

145428 Goods van, 1944.

146366 'Van' plywood, 1948; in this case the plywood refers to the material used in construction.

S4409 6-wheeled milk tank, 1931.

950592 'Toad' 20t brake van, 1950.

Chapter Five

Rebuilds and Replicas

The aim of the Society has always been to preserve as complete a collection of different types of GWR locomotive and rolling stock as possible. It is, however, an inevitable part of the historical process that many classes will have become obsolete over time and been discarded so that no examples remain for restoration. So if there are historically important machines that no longer exist, then the only solution is to build them. It would be possible to recreate a near-perfect replica by starting from scratch and manufacturing every single part. This is an expensive solution to the problem, but fortunately there is an alternative; transform existing locomotives into examples of the lost classes. Inevitably, not every part will be available but important structures can be based very largely on engines that are themselves unlikely ever to be restored because of their condition. This is an altogether more attractive and less costly solution to the problem. When does a newly created locomotive become a replica and when is it a rebuild? It doesn't really matter, as long as the finished product is right and fit for purpose.

One fascinating class of vehicle had indeed long since gone out of service and, although no actual examples had survived in their original form, one at least was still present though transformed into something very different. Steam railmotors had been phased out by the middle of the 1930s but not destroyed. Many were converted into push-pull coaches. It was decided to take the bold step of reversing history; a push-pull coach would be turned back into a railmotor.

The idea of railmotors was not new when the GWR began manufacturing them. The earliest example was designed by James Samuel for the Eastern Counties Railway and built by W. Bridges Adam. They went on to develop a larger version, one of which went into service on the Bristol & Exeter Railway in 1848. Unlike later versions, it looked rather like a conventional locomotive, apart from its vertical boiler, which, instead of being coupled to its carriage was permanently attached. The idea was not taken up and railmotor development came to a halt in Britain. There were, however, developments in continental Europe, including a strange double-decker steam rail car built for the Hessian Ludwig Railway in Germany. But by the early twentieth century, the advantages of having a light self-propelled steam vehicle for use on branch lines and to serve small stations and halts was becoming more evident. The London & South Western Railway built a prototype, which was borrowed by the GWR for trials. They liked the concept and set out to develop their own version and as a result, 99 steam powered rail cars were produced between 1904 and 1908. The cars were only able to take one extra vehicle, and in practice it became normal to link them to autocoaches, as described in Chapter 2. This enabled them to be driven efficiently in both directions. Railmotor and autocoach thus formed a complete unit.

One advantage was that they were economical to run for local trains, but they were considerably less popular with maintenance staff. Before anything could be done, the entire unit had to be withdrawn and the vehicle taken out of service. On the other hand, it enabled the GWR to run trains to small halts that would otherwise scarcely warrant any sort of service. One of the routes that they served was on the main line to Cheltenham, serving stations between Stonehouse and Chalford. The latter was home to the railcar, but the facilities were primitive. Coal was kept in a wagon parked on a siding and the fireman had to move the fuel from the siding to the engine on a wheelbarrow. The same siding housed the gas tanker that was needed to supply the lighting. There was also a water source, but none of these facilities made life for the fireman much easier. Walter Cottam worked on the railmotors and he remembered just how difficult his life was. For a start, he had to forget everything he'd ever been taught about firing. Standard practice was to add coal with the regulator open, but on

The 4-wheel power bogie with its vertical boiler attached to the frame that will support the carriage compartment of the steam railmotor.

the railmotor if you did that it let a blast of cold air into the firebox with disastrous results. Consequently, he had to use every station stop for a burst of frantic firing to ensure he had enough steam for the next leg of the journey. Water capacity was equally inadequate, so for even a comparatively short trip it was necessary to top up at each end. Getting up on the footplate today – itself quite a struggle – takes you to an area totally different from any other cab. The boiler occupies virtually all the space in the middle of the cab, and there scarcely seems space for two on the footplate. There is also a unique problem; the controls are attached to the power bogie, which means they move as the machine goes round bends. It must have been something of a relief to the driver when he could retire to the comparative comfort of the cab in the auto-trailer at the other end of the train. The fireman, necessarily, had to stay where he was.

The idea was good, but in many ways, they were victims of their own success, attracting more passengers and business than the railmotor could cope with. So in practice, the cars were far from ideal, hence their abandonment and the change to using adapted locomotives, such as the 14xx with the autocoach. Between 1914 and 1935, all the railmotors were either scrapped or converted. Among those which had been converted into auto-trailers was railcar No 93 and this was the one that had been acquired by the Society and which would, it was hoped, be transformed back into its original incarnation. And the project included the restoration of auto-trailer No 92 so that they could be run together just as they would have been in the early twentieth century.

The first stage was to assess just what work needed to be done and that involved stripping down the vehicles to discover how much original material could still be used and what would need to be manufactured. Once that long process had been completed, it was possible to assess the likely costs and quantity of work required. It was immediately obvious that this was a major undertaking that required massive funding. It was not a project that the Society could expect to undertake using only its own resources and volunteers, nor was it one they could expect to finance from donations from friends and enthusiasts. The most likely source of funding was the National Lottery; a bid was prepared in 2006 and, with an admirable disregard for superstition, the actual day of submission was a Friday 13th – it was successful. The project that had been referred to as one of the most important in railway preservation history had the green light.

Converting the former autocarriage back into a steam railcar involved two quite different operations. The simpler of the two was turning the passenger section back into its original form. The second involved creating an entirely new power unit. The latter was one part of the process that was too much to undertake at Didcot with a volunteer workforce and could only have been achieved slowly and at the expense of virtually all other projects. So the work went instead to the workshops of the Llangollen Railway. The two vehicles had a short run out on the main line behind an EWS class 66 locomotive, from Didcot down to the freight terminal at Milton, where they were placed on low loaders for the trip to Wales. The long work of creating the steam railmotor and trailer could get under way, but it would not be simple. For a start, finding all the right components for a faithful restoration was always going to be tricky, but help arrived very early on from an unexpected quarter.

The railmotor and the trailer were both fitted with 'walkover' seats. This form of seating was common in trams. The seat backs are pivoted, so that when the tram arrived at one terminus, they could all be pushed over. As a result, passengers always faced the front, whichever direction the tram was travelling. By an extraordinary piece of good fortune, walkover seats to exactly the right specification were available, having been scrapped from a tramway. But this was not here in Britain; it was the Glenoig Tramway of Southern Australia. The trams may have been run on the other side of the world, but the seats were made by Peters of Slough. It was two Australian GWS members, John Moore and Reg Watters, who discovered them and there were just enough there to fit out both vehicles. They arrived back in Britain in July 2016. It was a promising start to the rebuilding programme.

The job of building the vertical unit for the power unit went to Israel Newton of Bradford, a company that had been making boilers since 1803. On 11 January 2007, the great day arrived when the boiler would be steamed for the first time. A large deputation arrived from Didcot to witness this important stage in the reconstruction programme: the project engineer, Dennis Howells; Richard Croucher and Graham Drew from the project team; and Adrian Knowles and Andy Hook to look after the publicity. The day was a great success and the final step was to test the safety valves under high pressure. With everything in order, the boiler was drained and everything dried out ready for its journey south to be united with the power bogie at the Tyseley Locomotive Works in Birmingham.

When it came to completing the bogie, there were several pressing problems to overcome, not least the fact that several essential components did not exist at all. The only solution was to make them, and this involved having patterns made so that they could be cast. The largest item was the main steam pipe, an inverted fork supplying the two pistons. There were problems to be overcome and on occasions it seemed that it would be up to the modern engineers to try and work out what had originally been done without the benefit of any working drawings. This was done for the valve gear and a wooden mock-up prepared. By a fortunate coincidence, while this was being done, researchers at the National Railway Museum, who had been looking for drawings for the very different County project, found a set of railmotor drawings, fragile tracings but still very clear. To everyone's relief, it was now clear that the mock-up was perfectly in keeping with the original plans. By the end of November, the boiler and power bogie had been united and the intention was to take the completed assembly to Didcot for display before being sent off to Llangollen. Eventually, the completed power bogie was tested out on the tracks at Llangollen. It was an amazing sight, looking for all the world like a giant tea urn on the move, enveloped in smoke and steam.

In the meantime, work was continuing on the railmotor body. In effect, it had to be more or less dismembered. The main body was lifted from the frame and the bogies removed from the underframe. The latter had to be shot blasted to provide clean metal surfaces where any fault could easily be seen and rectified and the body was set up on frames so that all parts could be inspected and worked on. The railmotor also needed to be supplied with a temporary bogie to replace the one removed to form the power bogie – otherwise it could not have been moved on its own wheels. There are two over-riding criteria for all this kind of restoration work; it must be done to create a finished vehicle as close to the original as possible, and it has to pass the rigorous tests that will allow it to be declared safe enough to go into service.

Early in 2008, work was progressing on the underframe and trailing bogie. It was impossible to see exactly what condition the bogie was in because of the grime that had encrusted it over the years. So, as with the frame, the first requirement was to shot blast it to get down to the metal and one pleasing feature emerged from under the grime; the wheels were still stamped with the GWR monogram. It is always good to know that you have got down to

The completed steam railmotor at work on the Looe branch line.

original fittings. What was less satisfactory was to discover quite a lot of charring on the frame. This dates back to October 1974, when a crew were at Didcot having just got back from the first vintage train run. They were relaxing in one of the coaches, when they received the very alarming news that the coach appeared to be on fire. The fire brigade was called in and in the meantime, one of the coach windows had been smashed in and a hose from a fire hydrant pushed through. By the time the brigade arrived it was mostly under control, and the culprit was soon identified; a frying pan had been left on a gas ring. At the time it seemed that only superficial damage had been done, but now years later it was clear that the fire had only just been caught in time, before the whole carriage went up in flames, probably taking much of the rolling stock and the shed with it. It was a sobering discovery.

There was a great deal of work to be done. Everything needed to be overhauled; springs needed to be re-tempered and the underframe levelled but at least some items, such as the sand boxes, turned out to be in perfectly good condition. In the meantime, there were a lot of parts to be ordered, ranging from vacuum gauges to special cloth for the roller blinds, manufactured in Holland. As well as dealing with the underframe and bogies, the main carriage frame also had to be inspected, and a great deal of the timber replaced. Another unexpected discovery was that Swindon works were not always the seat of perfection that has often been claimed for them. The team had the original drawings and specifications, but when they were compared with the actual vehicle, discrepancies were discovered. As drawings come before construction, it can safely be assumed that the original work was not quite as accurate as it might have been. On the other hand, taking a more pragmatic approach, everything worked, which is what really mattered. But it gave the restoration team quite a few headaches.

In January 2009, the new power unit bogie was united with the original 70ft long 1908 refurbished underframe. This was a more complex affair than it would have been with a more conventional set up. Because the boiler sits at the point where the normal pivot would be situated, the power bogie used the Dean 'centreless' system. Basically, the carriage is held on two scroll arms at the sides of the frame, which in turn rest on two beams suspended under the bogie by springs. Needless to say, as no one had used this system for over a century there was no one on site who had ever worked on such an assembly before, so there were anxious moments when the work was completed and was first put to the test. Once the whole assembly was completed, it was moved out and given a run to see if it really would go round curves without any parts fouling. It was a success and only minimum adjustments needed to be made.

In November 2010, the day had finally arrived when everything could come together. The engine had been tried and not found wanting. The carriage was jacked up and the accommodation bogie removed to allow the power unit to be put in place. There still had to be running trials of the complete unit at Llangollen, but now it was possible to announce that passengers would be able to ride in the railmotor at the Bank Holiday in May 2012. It would be the first time a GWR railmotor had been out on the tracks with paying passengers since 1935. It had been a long process, involving a lot of hard work and a great deal of money, but the end product justified the effort. The railmotor was not to be limited to running at Didcot, but was to be available for use on other lines at various times, so that rail enthusiasts all over Britain might have the chance to see this unique vehicle. In June 2012, an important landmark was passed when the railmotor was certified for main line running. That year it was taken down to Cornwall for running on the former Liskeard and Looe Railway.

It had always been the intention to run the railmotor in conjunction with the autotrailer, just as it had been in the past to create a two-carriage unit that could be driven in either direction from either end. Bringing the trailer up to standard was a more conventional restoration job, but still involved a great deal of work, notably in providing hundreds of feet of hardwood moulding for both the interior and exterior. The sliding doors had to be replaced. When the coach had been simply used for accommodation it seems that dartboards had been stuck on the door and, judging by the number of holes, used by very inexpert players. The work was eventually completed and the combined vehicles were able to run again.

The railmotor is something of an oddity among engines of the steam age but there are also a number of important examples of more conventional locomotives that have not survived into the present age. In the case of the broad gauge period, the only answer is to build replicas – and these are dealt with in the chapter on the broad gauge. But a very important period in the history of the railway was that immediately following the final abandonment of the broad gauge in 1892. At the start of the twentieth century, the GWR went through a period of modernisation that included a complete reassessment of the needs for new fast express locomotives for use on the extensive network. The process started under William Dean, but on his retirement, the task of devising new locomotives went to his former assistant, now Chief Mechanical Engineer, George Jackson Churchward. In order to work out the best way forward, a number of different locomotive designs were inspected, including engines developed in France and America. As a result of this process, decisions were reached on several design features and a first prototype was introduced in 1902 with a 4-6-0 wheel arrangement, parallel boiler with no dome, Belpaire firebox and two large outside cylinders. A second prototype soon followed, this time with a tapering boiler, modified valve gear and with steam pressure raised from 200 to 225psi. A third prototype was altered to a 4-4-2 arrangement to enable comparisons to be made – based on a French compound. When the series went into production in 1905, they were the most advanced locomotives of their day. Their performance depended on the combination of large boiler capacity and wide steam ports to serve the large 18in x 30in cylinders. The Class was numbered 2900 and known by the name of 'Saints'. They were to prove remarkably effective and remained the principal express locomotives until the introduction of the Castles in the early 1920s, but many continued in service long after this – the last Saint was only retired in 1953.

Such a vital link between the broad gauge and standard gauge eras clearly deserved a place in the Didcot collection, but sadly this class was one of the non-survivors. There was, however, a possible solution – convert one of the preserved locomotives into a Saint. That may sound a somewhat strange notion, but there is a very sound historical precedent. When Charles Collett took over from Churchward, he began developing a number of new classes. In 1924, he adapted a Saint Class, a change that among other things involved reducing the size of the drive wheels from 6ft 8½in diameter to 6ft, creating the prototype Hall. So if Collett could turn a Saint into a Hall, why couldn't the Society turn a Hall back into a Saint? In 1971, Peter Rich of the South Wales Group suggested that there were enough bits and pieces at Barry to convert into a Saint, but at the time it seemed just a little too ambitious and would make too great a demand on available funds. Nevertheless, it was agreed that this would be an excellent project and over the next three years the situation began to look more favourable. With the price of scrap metal being likely to rise with the arrival of what was then the new tax, VAT, it seemed sensible to buy a locomotive – and even if the Saint project didn't come to fruition, it could still be restored and nothing would be lost. So, in 1974, thanks to a loan from a member, the Society purchased 4942 *Maindy Hall* from Barry for the project with the idea of using it to recreate a Saint in its final incarnation, which included a frame with elegant curves at the cab end and over the cylinders. This was thought to be just too complicated – and many thought the whole project was a step too far for the Society. However, the work done on restoring *King Edward II*, that involved manufacturing a whole new set of drive wheels, proved that they were capable of carrying through a major project. Nevertheless, it was decided to go for the slightly less ambitious plan of creating an earlier version of a Saint, with a straight frame.

Moving the Hall to Didcot was not straightforward. The motion was dismantled and sent ahead by road, the intention being to move the locomotive itself by rail but the bogie and tender axle box keeps had been removed and the axle journals had rusted. So remedial work was essential. By this time, the Society had acquired three other locomotives waiting to be moved – 3738, 4144 and 7202 – so it made sense to move the four together as a single train. The procession set off headed by a Class 47 diesel at a stately 25mph with regular inspection stops. All went well as far as Swindon when a hot box was discovered on 4942's tender. The bearing was refitted and the tender had to be jacked up nine times before everything was declared to be in proper working order. *Maindy Hall* arrived at Didcot on the early evening of 20 April 1974 and work on the Saint project could get under way.

The aim was to stay as close as possible to original Churchward design features, though this was not always possible. For example, a new cab had to be constructed, but the original would have had a timber roof and that would not meet modern design standards, so a steel roof had to be added instead. Other features of the cab such as the footplate platform could be constructed using parts from the Hall. The good news was that a new copper firebox had been fitted in a major overhaul at Swindon just 2½ years before 4942 was retired from service. The boiler would have to be given a complete overhaul and some changes were needed, including using countersunk rivets to replace the original for the smokebox. Some changes needed were more or less cosmetic but were essential to give the same appearance as those of the Saint, such as adding a tall cover to the safety valve but removing the protective shield from

The steam railmotor coupled to an autocoach, a common working practice. In this view we are looking at the driver's cab on the autocoach.

the whistle. A chimney from a Grange or modified Hall would be needed as a close approximation to the Saint chimney. The frame would need adaptation which would involve forging an extension for the front end.

Although parts from the Hall could be used or adapted, in many cases there were a number of components that would have to be manufactured. Major items included the drive wheels, where it was hoped some existing Castle wheels could be used. New cylinders would also have to be manufactured to replicate the 1912 version with 18½in bore. There were many other details that needed to be changed and some non-ferrous parts might need remaking. It was decided to have a 3,500 gallon tender and at the early stages it was not clear whether this would be an adaptation or a new build. This is only a summary of the work that would be needed, with many details omitted, but it was clear that this was going to be a long process, involving a great deal of work and an equally large amount of fund raising. A team was assembled, including Peter Rich, who had first suggested the idea, Peter Chapman as overall project leader and in charge of looking after the cylinder construction programme, with Dennis Howells and Mike Rudge having responsibility for the wheels. Richard Croucher had the possibly less exciting, but absolutely essential, task of raising the money.

There are a number of possible starting points for reconstruction when no actual originals exist. One source is old photographs, but these provide only limited information and generally only show external features. Working drawings are a far superior source but these too have their limitations. There is often a lot of essential information that is simply not there: what were the engineering tolerances; what materials were used; how were parts manufactured – cast or forged – and so on. Turning original drawings into modern drawings that have all the necessary information for present-day manufacturers is a skilled and difficult task, but fortunately two members were up to the job – Mike Rudge and Peter Rich. They spent literally thousands of hours producing the essential drawings. Sadly, Peter Rich died in 2014, not living long enough to see his dream fulfilled.

When creating one class of locomotive out of another, there are bound to be difficulties when dimensions change. The drive wheels of the Hall are 6ft in diameter while those of the Saint need to be 6ft 8½in. The drive wheels would have to be manufactured. Originally, it had been hoped to use Castle bogie wheels but these proved to be cracked so that was another manufacturing job. The positive side to this was that they could be Churchward design rather than Collett and original drawings existed. Incorporating the larger driving wheels meant adjustments to the frame would have to be made and it was decided to go for new cylinders rather than trying to adapt 4942's. There were no drawings for Saint cylinders available but there was a drawing for the similar cylinders for a County. Fortunately, the right hand and left hand cylinders are identical, so the same casting pattern could be used for both of them. Even so, manufacturing a whole new wheel set and cylinders was going to be a very expensive business. Because of the increased size of the drive wheels, the frame was now higher than it had been originally, and that meant that there would now be a greater clearance above the bogie. Rather than rebuild the bogie frame, it was decided to put in a spacer plate. This allowed the Hall bogie to be reused and is not an obvious deviation from the original Saint design. There were all kinds of details that needed to be attended to, such as replacing all the brass beading that had been removed during the First World War.

In 1995, manufacturing the new parts could get under way. Patterns had to be prepared for casting the drive wheels. The central pair have larger bosses in the middle than the other two pairs, so a pattern was made for these first, which could then be modified for the others. A new pattern was also required for the bogie wheels, all the work being carried out at the William Cook foundry. The axles were forged at Adtranz of Derby and tyres came from South Africa. Machining work was carried out by Bootham Engineering and tyre assembly was completed at Eastleigh. Altogether it was a complex business co-ordinating so many different aspects of the job. Preparing the patterns for the new cylinders was even more complicated than it was for the wheels and it was decided to cast just one in the first place to make sure everything worked out. The foundry was James W. Shenton of Tipton, who experienced no problems at all; a tribute to the pattern makers. Machining was again undertaken by Bootham and piston valve liners were made and fitted at the Severn Valley Railway.

With work well under way, the next stage was the extensive modification needed on the frame. It was obvious that this was beyond the resources available at Didcot, so in 2002, the frame and new cylinders were sent up to Riley and Son at Bury.

The job of constructing the extension frame went to John Heasketh, also in Bury. The first task at Riley's was a non-destructive test to locate cracks, which were then repaired, before the main task of modification got under way. This involved a great deal of toing and froing between Bury and Didcot to check on details. By 2004, the frame extension was complete but work at Riley's slowed down due to their many other commitments.

In the meantime, work was steadily going forward at Didcot. Work on the bogie was completed and the tubes were removed from the boiler to make it easier to move. The new wheelsets were also now complete and everything was sent up to Bury for assembly in July 2005. Inevitably there were problems to be solved with some parts, but by the time all necessary adjustments had been made, frame and wheels were united and a 4-6-0 was taking shape. There were still problems to be solved, including the construction of the very complex motion bracket that was in use on the original Saints. An effort was made to make a pattern for casting, but in the event, it proved just too complex. How, one wonders, was it made over a century ago? The decision was made to use the original motion bracket from the Hall. The rocking lever bearing, which had originally been integral with the rest of the bracket, could now be cast separately, a comparatively straightforward job, and the two sections then united. Reconstruction often involves a degree of pragmatism, finding solutions that work rather than attempting a 100 per cent accurate replica of the original model.

By September 2006, the time had come to fit the boiler to the frame. Inevitably, there were adjustments needed but no problems appeared that weren't reasonably easy to solve. In October 2006, the whole assembly was towed up and down the yard at Bury and declared fit to be transported by rail. On 6 November, it arrived back at Didcot. The locomotive had been given a number – 2999 – but originally had no name. Various suggestions were put forward and the final decision was taken by a ballot of the members. She was to be *Lady of Legend*.

There was still an immense amount of work to be done. With the boiler tubes removed, a thorough inspection was possible that revealed a few faults that had to be corrected, which involved some major replacements – notably all the steel stays and the front tubeplate. It was decided to replace all non-ferrous fittings, but in the interests of authenticity there was a hunt for original parts. Most preserved locomotives had parts manufactured to designs introduced after the Churchward era, so finding originals was no easy matter. Members kindly donated a chimney and safety valve bonnet, which could be successfully adapted while other components came from a variety of sources – the vacuum gauge was bought at an auction and the steam heat gauge was bought on eBay. How astonished Churchward would have been to hear that an item he designed had been bought via a computer – and probably impressed. Where originals were not available, replacements had to be cast, usually involving the use of patterns held at Didcot.

There was also much work to be done to prepare the boiler for its steam test, including replacing boiler tubes and new stays for the firebox. To reunite the boiler with the firebox, flush riveting was to be used as it was in Churchward's day. In effect, this was a complete major overhaul. The steampipes to connect the cylinders to the boiler had to be remade. It was a complex casting, but fortunately there was an existing casting at Tyseley, which was sent on loan to Didcot so that a pattern could be made. This was just the start of assembling all the different components that would be needed to create a fully operational Saint. In working on the motion, it was discovered that one of the connecting rods was stamped with the number 2906. This meant that it had been used on *Lady of Lynn.* So there is one part at least of *Lady of Legend* that had actually been on a Saint. The long process of making new parts and refurbishing old continued through the years. It was, of course, not just the locomotive that needed to be constructed; it needed an equally accurate tender. A Churchward 3,500 gallon tank was purchased, but many parts were missing, so that too required a great deal of work.

The general public got their first view of the locomotive in July 2013, when it was wheeled out for display on No 2 turntable. The gang had been hard at work on the left hand side of the engine – the one that would be seen by the visitors. The cab, splashers and smokebox had been painted and the brass beading, number plate and nameplate had been added. It may not yet have become a fully operational Saint, but now at least it looked like one. The tender, however, was still very far from completion and remained in the workshop. By now, most of the major components were available, whether manufactured or refurbished but there was still an immense amount of work to be done. There were tasks, such as fitting in all the pipework to the cab, that were described by Peter Chapman as 'fiddly', which is perhaps an understatement, but by

2017 the end was finally in sight. The fund was still £30,000 short of the amount needed for completion – but the group were allowed to overdraw to see the project through. That year, Timeline Events asked if they could paint the *Lady* black for a special photo shoot event. Although anathema to some it was an opportunity to put the engine on show – and it could be treated as an undercoat until the correct livery was applied. But she would not be shown with her new name and number until properly dressed in green. A very important stage was reached in November 2017, when the boiler passed its steam test and could now be united with the smokebox and assembled on the frame. At the time of writing there is still work to be done, but the *Lady of Legend* could be dancing down the tracks in the not too distant future.

There was another important gap in the collection. The final stage in the development of the design features pioneered in the Saints came at the very end of the Second World War in 1945. Frederick Hawksworth was now the man in charge and it had long been an ambition of his to design a Pacific for fast passenger services, but the

The partially completed reconstruction of a Saint, *Lady of Legend*, on show at Didcot with *Hinderton Hall.*

war years had intervened and the project had to be shelved, There was, however, a need for a powerful mixed traffic engine that could cope with the severe gradients in the west of the region. So he set to work on a new 4-6-0 that was to become the 10xx County Class. He introduced several features that had been developed for the Modified Halls. Previously the Great Western had, like other major companies, followed their own independent lines of development but in the war years it had been necessary to spread manufacturing for maximum efficiency. Hawksworth had the opportunity to study the 8F boiler introduced by Stanier into LMS locomotives, and he was sufficiently impressed to incorporate it into his new design. Other changes included increasing boiler pressure to 280psi – though this was reduced later in working practice – and adding a double chimney. He also saw the engine as a test bed for trying out ideas that he could incorporate into his planned Pacific – but, sadly for him, the Pacific was destined to remain on the drawing board. The appeal of having both the earliest version of the 4-6-0 two outside cylinder engine and its final form was obvious.

A Society member, David Bradshaw, suggested that among the locomotives still left from the Barry scrapyard, which were in too poor a condition to be worth restoring, there would be enough bits and pieces to create a County. The final ten locomotives left at the yard had originally been intended to form the basis for a railway centre in Cardiff, but that plan folded. As a result, there were three locomotives still owned by Cardiff and seven in the care of the Vales of Glamorgan. The idea was that all ten should be disposed of and negotiations got under way. Those negotiations dragged on for an incredible time, almost eight years before agreement was reached. The final document allowed for the creation of a Hawksworth County 4-6-0, a Churchward County 4-4-0 and a 47xx 2-8-0, as well as providing parts for other organisations considering building a County and a Grange. An appeal for funds for creating a County was opened with encouraging results and by July 2005, £85,000 had been raised, enough to make a start. The first job was to arrange for six new drive wheels to be prepared. This would involve making a pattern, casting the wheels and forging the axles and crank pins. The estimated cost was £120,000. It was decided to ask for spoke sponsorship; as each wheel had 21 spokes that made a grand total of 126 so £1,000 per spoke would cover the entire cost. The Vale of Glamorgan Council who offered Hall No 7927 and an 8F boiler made an important donation. It had always been the intention to run the completed County on other lines, not just at Didcot. So as a way of saying thank you to the Council a guarantee was offered that when completed it would spend time on the Vales of Glamorgan Railway – and would be graced with the name *County of Glamorgan*. Unfortunately, just three years later, the Council decided to remove its support from the Railway and offered the site to a new commercial venture, which would eventually become the Barry Tourist Railway. Three other locomotives were acquired to be scavenged for parts for the GWS and other projects – 4115, 2861 and 5227. The latter, once the useful parts were removed, was brought to Didcot where, as mentioned earlier, it was put on display. It gives a good idea of why these engines were basically beyond salvation. They were, however, all to prove extremely valuable in rebuild programmes.

By November, the modified Hall was leaving Barry for Llangollen, where it was to be dismantled and the frames sand blasted. Meanwhile the bogie, which had already been removed, was sent to Bill Parker's Flourmill Works where the wheels would be turned and the journals polished before sending on to Didcot. The good news was that the boiler from the London Midland Region Stanier 8F which had been sent to L&NWR Co. Ltd was found to be in excellent condition. It was also found that the dimensions were remarkably close to those needed for a County; the greatest discrepancy was a very modest $^1/_{32}$ in. As always in these projects, some extra work was required; the front of the boiler had to be replaced to fit County length and a new smoke box and front tubeplate would be needed. The original had been fitted with a dome, which was not required, so the holes had to be blanked out. Altogether, the work needed was less than anticipated and, which was equally good news, the estimated cost would be a lot less as well. Some work could be carried out at Didcot by volunteers, including providing a new cab. As fund raising for the project was proceeding at a good pace, everything seemed set for a bright future; as a piece in the Newsletter put it, wheel sets should be provided 'without delay'. The forecast was to prove more than a little optimistic.

The saga of the wheels was long and drawn out. At first, they were promised for spring, then September 2010. In May 2011, the *Echo* report on progress recorded that although they had been promised by 1 March, they were still not quite ready, as the eccentrics had not been fitted nor lead poured for the balance weights. But at least, in theory, the end was in sight and they would be soon at Didcot.

One problem was that the work involved a whole variety of different stages. It started with William Cook's of Sheffield preparing the patterns and casting all six wheels. The axles and tyres came from South Africa and then the wheels and axles were sent to the Riley works for assembly. When that was completed, they went down to the South Devon Railway's workshops for the tyres to be shrunk on. Then it was back to Riley's, which was where the final stages were being completed. It had all been rather frustrating, as without the wheels, it was impossible to complete other tasks such as machining the axle boxes - and moving the frame around the workshop was a tricky business that would be far, far simpler with wheels in place. The good news, however, was that work was going ahead on forging parts for the outside motion. Two connecting rods had already been sponsored and a short-term loan had been offered by a member for the four coupling rods so as a result, work could go ahead on forging and machining all six.

As well as work being carried out by contractors, a lot was going ahead with work parties at Didcot, with welders and riveters hard at work on different parts of both the locomotive and tender. That year, a party went down to Barry to spend three rather sweaty days stripping usable parts off 5227. As the report in the *Echo* pointed out, progress might seem slow to outsiders, but it was reliant on volunteers. And there were many stages to go through. For example, with components such as the front dragbox, a new casting would be needed. That meant first of all researching and preparing drawings, then finding a pattern maker and finally getting a foundry to do the actual casting. This is not only time consuming but also costs a lot of money, so fund raising has to go in step with the actual work. Understandably, things do not always move on at the speed that had been planned. It had been hoped that re-wheeling would be completed in 2014, but after inspecting the horns and the work that would be needed, it was decided that instead of being done at Didcot, it would make more sense to send the horns for regrinding together with overhaul of the axle boxes to the locomotive works at Tyseley. Somewhat frustratingly, this meant undoing some of the work already completed in order to send the frames out from Didcot. Tyseley was also going to be grinding the valve chests.

If work on the wheels didn't go to plan, at least other items on the agenda were more successful. Huge progress was made on the construction of the tender. By the summer of 2015, Tyseley had finished their work and the frames were back at Didcot and

the firebox had been manufactured at Crewe. The long-awaited re-wheeling could now get under way, but not quite immediately. The date set for this momentous event was 23 April 2016. Perhaps inevitably, there would be one more hiccup before the work was completed. The centre drivers were gradually raised into position and the axle boxes proved to be a perfect fit with the hornblocks. Unfortunately, when it came to the leading drivers, things did not go so well and the axle boxes kept sticking. It was decided that further investigation was needed to find out how to remedy the situation. It was 21 May before the work was completed and the transformation was complete; the 4-4-0 was at long last a 4-6-0. From now on, the work could go steadily forward. The end would not be immediate but was very definitely in sight, and at the time of writing it is months rather than years away.

When the various locomotives from the Barry ten were acquired, there was always the idea that one day a third rebuild would be possible – a 47xx. Churchward's first 2-8-0 locomotives, the 28xx class, were designed as long ago as 1903. By 1919, he had revised

Work in progress in creating a County Class, by adding an extra pair of wheels to the frame from a modified Hall.

the design, with larger driving wheels and a larger boiler. They were originally designed for mixed traffic, especially for heavy, fast freight, but were later to prove their worth as passenger locomotives. Only nine of the class were built – 4700 to 4708. It was decided to construct 4709, which would fill another of the gaps in the collection and was a locomotive that many in the Society were especially keen to see brought back to life. It was decided that this time, the main construction work would take place at Llangollen.

Work got under way in 2010, with Paul Carpenter as project manager. The first step was to bring 4115 to the works and dismantle it. The front end of the frame, apart from the cylinder blocks, was very similar to that of a 47xx and could be used. A new main frame, 31ft 1in long, had to be constructed. The steel was rolled and profiled at the Tata works in South Wales then sent to TM Engineering at Kingswinsford in the Black Country, where it was machined and drilled with over 200 holes. Three rather rusty wheels came off 4115 and were sent to the South Devon Railway for refurbishment, while the fourth set of drive wheels were being manufactured. In the meantime, 5227 was brought to Llangollen to provide axle boxes, horns and the essential fourth axle to take the new set of driving wheels. Llangollen ordered a new machine for grinding the horns to help the process along. As will be obvious from the history of the Saint and County rebuilds, this will be a long process, depending on a whole variety of factors, especially the size of the workforce available and the all-important one of having money in the bank. Rebuilding locomotives into new configurations is always an expensive affair, but seeing a locomotive appear that was thought to be gone for ever makes it all worthwhile – it is rather like the railway equivalent of Jurassic Park, if a good deal more practical.

That is not quite the end of the story. The Great Western Society is not the only organisation that saw the Barry cast offs as being capable of transformation into a new locomotive, where none of that class has survived. The Betton Grange Society in Llangollen has been beavering away, as the name suggests, in recreating a Grange. In 2016, as the project was nearing completion, they announced that, when it wasn't out on main line duty, they would like it to have a home base at Didcot. Needless to say the suggestion met an enthusiastic reception. When the restoration movement first got under way, would anyone have believed that one day it might be possible to see a Saint, a County and a Grange lined up outside their engine shed in the twenty-first century?

CHAPTER SIX

Broad Gauge

The one thing that most people remember about Brunel's Great Western is that he set his rails nominally 7 feet apart (in practice 7ft ¼in) instead of the 4ft 8½in selected by George Stephenson. It is not too difficult to understand Brunel's reasoning. As was explained in Chapter 1, Stephenson had not really chosen his gauge as being the most suitable. His first locomotives had been designed to run on existing tramways at mines. Having begun by designing locomotives to this gauge, when he became chief engineer for the much more important Liverpool & Manchester Railway, a genuine intercity line that placed as much emphasis on passenger traffic as it did on freight, he saw no reason to make any changes. He had successfully run what was then the fastest locomotive ever built, *Rocket*, on the old gauge. The system worked well so why mess about with it? Brunel started from a very different position.

The Great Western was to be built to link what was then one of the country's busiest ports, Bristol, to the capital. So Brunel ignored what had been going on in the rest of Britain and asked a pertinent question. What would be the ideal system that would ensure trains travelled as rapidly as possible and offered passengers the greatest degree of comfort? He decided that what he rather contemptuously referred to as 'the coal wagon gauge' was inadequate. But he went even further; he decided that everything about the permanent way would be different from all its predecessors. He devised a route that would aim to be as flat as a billiard table and was convinced that for smooth running, the track should be as rigidly fixed as possible. He was also unimpressed by the rails currently in use on other lines; where it had been common practice to use wrought iron rails that looked a little like dumbbells in cross section, Brunel opted for 'bridge' rails that looked very different. The sides were flat but rose up in a U-shape in the middle. And the method of fixing the rails was equally new.

As late as the 1820s, railways such as the S&DR were still mounting their rails on stone blocks; this allowed space for horses to pass down the middle. With the advent of the L&MR and the abandonment of any use of horses, this system became obsolete and

The arrival of the working replica of Gooch's *Iron Duke* is celebrated at Didcot: the replica was built by a Science Museum team, led by Tony Hall Patch.

railways began to be built with the rails laid on transverse wooden sleepers, and held in place by iron chairs. Brunel used timber under the rails, but his was a baulk railway in which the timber ran the full length of the rail. The baulks were made out of heavy pine faced with a hardwood. They were secured in place by metal ties, running right across both sets of lines on the double track railway. These cross members were further strengthened by metal spikes driven into the roadbed. Once this rigid three-dimensional framework was in place, the whole system was ballasted.

Modern engineering opinion is that the Brunel system was, if anything, too rigid; there needed to be a certain amount of play in the rails. There were trials to try and determine which system was best but it was really impossible to tell whether differences in performance were down to the track or the locomotives using it. But as the system spread, the break in gauge between the Stephenson and the Brunel became a matter of growing concern. It was a source of irritation to passengers and a headache for operators when everything had to be changed from one system to the other at places where they met. The decision as to which system should prevail was never really in doubt and had very little to do with the intrinsic merits of the system. The Stephenson system was by now so much more extensive than the Great Western that economics demanded that it was chosen to become the standard gauge for Britain. There was an interim period during which the broad gauge was given a third intermediate rail to allow the tracks to be used by locomotives from other regions. All that came to an end in May 1892, when the very last broad gauge train ran and the last of the wide track was removed. Sections of the old bridge rail are still to be seen around the country, having been acquired for all kinds of purposes, often appearing in country areas as fence and gate posts. But as far as the railways were concerned, Brunel's beloved broad gauge was no more. Fortunately, that turned out to be not quite true – there were important bits to be found in different parts of the system.

If Didcot was to truly represent Great Western history, then the period of over half a century when the broad gauge was in use could not be ignored. The question was – how could this be achieved? It was known that there was no chance of getting an original broad gauge locomotive to put on display and it seemed equally unlikely that there would be sufficient track remaining anywhere to make it usable in any meaningful way. This was where members of the Taunton group came to the rescue. They discovered large sections of bridge rail had survived in a quarry at Burlescombe, just north of the main line near Tiverton in Devon. The quarry had originally been served by the less-than-successful Grand Western Canal, but the coming of the railway brought an immediate change and it was then served by the Westleigh Mineral Railway – and it was the remains of that line that the group had discovered.

In the winter of 1978, they began the task of uncovering the remains and salvaging track and points, which they brought back to Taunton for storage. Altogether some 17 to 18 tons of rail were recovered. The idea now was eventually to establish a broad gauge section at Didcot, but the plan was to represent it in its later form as mixed gauge. There was a very good reason for this decision. At the time there were no broad gauge locomotives to run on it and no one imagined that there ever would be.

The quarry is still worked and in 1983 a digger unearthed more rail. The Taunton group got into action again and this time wrote a fairly full account of their work in the GWS Newsletter. They spent several weekends clearing away spoil and foliage to expose the tracks. The work was given the name 'Operation Encore', because it was a repeat performance of what had been done five years before. The rails were released from the sleepers and dragged to a point where they could be loaded onto a lorry. A suitable vehicle was supplied by Taunton Cider and twenty-five volunteers turned up for the loading. It was just as well that there were so many as there was no crane and no lifting device of any kind to help with the work. It was quite a challenge, with 12½ tons of rail waiting to be lifted five feet up to the back of the truck and it all had to be done by hand. You would imagine at the end of that, that the volunteers would retire, satisfied with a job well done. There were two rails still left, buried under about three feet of spoil and tangled up with tree roots. Deciding that it would be mad to leave them there, they set to work and by nightfall there was approximately sixty more foot of rail loaded up. Taunton Cider did more than just provide the lorry, they also offered storage space. Although it is not mentioned in the Newsletter, it would be good to think that at the end of expending so much effort, the volunteers added to Taunton Cider's profits by the glassful.

When it came to assess what had been recovered, it was discovered that although the quarry company had taken away a great number of straight rails that they could use for all kinds of structures, they had left behind the invaluable switching points. This made it possible to lay out a really interesting broad gauge section back at Didcot. As Richard Antliff, the civil engineering manager, pointed out, the essential rule for all work done on the ground at Didcot is that it is done from a clear and well researched understanding of GWR practices.

The actual design was the work of a mechanical engineer, David Hartland, who wanted to demonstrate the different features of a mixed gauge railway. In particular, he wanted to show how a train 'side stepped' from one set of broad gauge tracks to the next. At one end of the system was the former transfer shed. There was a period in the history of the GWR when the broad gauge met the Stephenson gauge, and it was necessary to move material from one system to the other. This happened at Didcot, where the main line was broad, but the line to Oxford and onwards to Birmingham was standard gauge. So Didcot had a transfer shed, where loads could be exchanged under cover. It had a central platform, with broad gauge track to one side and standard gauge on the other. This became redundant in 1892 when the broad gauge years literally ended overnight but the structure remained in the station car park.

It was re-erected in 1980 at a period when the government had a plan to help young people find employment through the Manpower Services Commission. The scheme was a boon for voluntary organisations who now had access to a supply of free labour. The intention was that societies such as Didcot could get free labour and in return would help the volunteers acquire useful skills that would help them find jobs later. It was certainly successful as a means of getting a big and complex building re-erected on its new site, and today it forms the northern terminus of the branch line. Instead of freight, this would now be the terminus for the branch line and renamed 'Burlescombe' after the quarry that had made the whole scheme feasible. The idea was to leave from the platform in the transfer shed, go up over the layout, and then return back into the sidings. So the side stepping was strictly functional. The next stage was to delve back into history to see just how this had been done originally. It was the famous railway historian Charles Clinker who introduced Richard Antliff and David Hartland to the appropriate engineer and they were left alone in a room at

The replica of *Firefly* has been presented to the Society by the Firefly Trust, who were responsible for its construction.

Paddington overlooking Eastbourne Terrace, with a blackboard on an easel and a swathe of signed drawings by Brunel of Oxford, Wolverhampton and South Wales. They showed just how complex the operation had been, sometimes adding standard gauge to broad gauge and sometimes the other way round. The plans contained all the details that the team needed to create a baulk railroad at Didcot.

Once the layout had been designed, the drawings were all checked by an expert, John Mann, who was in charge of switch crossing at Bristol. The geometry of lines crossing on a curve is complex. Because the outer rails on a bend have a greater radius than the inner, they will all meet at different angles so there are four different Vs needed. By great good fortune, the lines brought back from Devon had exactly what was required, so work could begin in laying out the mixed grade track. Taunton still had a major part to play in the project, with gangs of four or five coming down once a month for weekends and working all hours, with, it seemed, very little chance of it ever being used other than by standard gauge stock. In fact, the very first run on any of the track during construction was by one of the most famous 'narrow gauge' locomotives of all time, a replica of Robert Stephenson's *Rocket*. This took place in September 1980 under the scrutiny of Mr Brunel; what the real Brunel would have thought of his beloved broad gauge being tested by his chief rival one can only imagine. He might even have been amused. After all, although he and Stephenson were engineering rivals, they were also close friends.

What the stalwarts who constructed this layout did not know at the time was that there were plans to create a replica broad gauge locomotive. The National Railway Museum decided that, with the help of the Friends of the Museum, it would be appropriate to have a replica to celebrate the GWR's 150th anniversary in 1985. The locomotive they chose was the *Iron Duke*, named after the war hero and later prime minister, the Duke of Wellington. It was a development by Daniel Gooch of his earlier locomotive *Fire Fly*, with a far larger boiler and a redesigned firebox. Originally, it had a single pair of leading wheels, but the weight proved too much so a second pair was added, giving it a (2+2)-2-2 configuration. It was a highly successful engine, completed at Swindon in 1847 and the first of a class of twenty-nine that continued in service, some only being retired in the 1870s. It took part in trials with the standard gauge engines of Stephenson and achieved an average speed of over 50mph and on one occasion was clocked at just over 78mph on a 1 in 100 downward slope. It was therefore an entirely appropriate locomotive to represent Gooch and the broad gauge at its very best. At the same time, replica second and third class coaches were constructed and they too now have a home at Didcot.

Unlike the *Rocket* replica, it was not built from scratch. It utilised the boiler, cylinder, valves, crank axle and inside frame from a J94 tank engine, one of many bought by the LNER from the War Department in 1946. As a result, not all the dimensions are the same as those of the original. The boiler is notably smaller; 10ft 2in long and 4ft 3in diameter against 11ft and 4ft 9¼in for the original. To some extent, this is a cosmetic job as the workers at Didcot discovered when they tried to move it using the buffer bars only to discover they were plywood not solid blocks of timber. Nevertheless, it looks splendid with its immense 8ft diameter drive wheels. It is now on more or less permanent loan from York and housed at Didcot. This was not the only replica planned for the celebrations. A group had got together to build a Firefly class locomotive.

The Firefly project had an unlikely start. It all began when architect John Mosse was asked by Bristol City Council to prepare drawings of the original Temple Meads station as British Rail were talking about making some drastic revisions to the layout. He duly went ahead and produced the drawings and then wondered if British Rail (Western Region) might not also like to have a set for their archives. He went up to Paddington and showed the work to the General Manager, Leslie Lloyd, who was suitably impressed and then asked John Mosse if he'd be interested in seeing Brunel's original drawings. Needless to say, this was not an offer he was ever likely to turn down. Large volumes of drawings were duly produced, and it was at this stage seeing so much material from the very beginning of the GWR story that a rather wild idea occurred to him. Wouldn't it be wonderful to recreate a broad gauge locomotive to celebrate the company's 150th birthday? And, as he lived in Bath at the time, what could be more appropriate than to run it from Brunel's original train shed to Bath and back. Clearly a full-sized replica could not run on standard gauge tracks, but he envisaged a three-quarter-size engine, capable of hauling a train of two or three replica carriages. Surprisingly perhaps, the idea was taken seriously by Leslie Lloyd and the wheels were set in motion.

The Firefly class of locomotives were designed by Gooch, but very largely based on the earlier locomotives supplied by the Robert Stephenson works in Newcastle, starting with *North Star.*

Seeing the two broad gauge replicas together highlights the design differences.

The Firefly locomotives, like the Stars, were 2-2-2s, with 7ft diameter drive wheels. Gooch, however, improved its steaming abilities by using a bigger boiler and a large Gothic domed firebox. The original *Fire Fly* was built by Jones, Taylor and Evans of Newton-le-Willows and delivered in 1840. Just five days after its arrival, it headed a directors' special train from Paddington to Reading and back and on the return it covered the 30¾ miles from Twyford to Reading in 37 minutes at an average speed of just under 50mph. It was a remarkable achievement for the time and a great tribute to the young engineer, who was just 24 years old. It is not difficult to see why recreating this remarkable engine would be greeted with enthusiasm by very many people – but not all.

With the encouragement of the Paddington officials, John Mosse went to Swindon, where it was hoped the replica might be built. There had been a slight change of plan. The idea now was to build a ⅔ scale version on the grounds that 4ft 8½in was almost exactly ⅔ of 7ft, so it should fit the existing tracks. It was also proposed to build a set of scaled down broad gauge carriages to complete the proposed passenger train. Once again, rather to John Mosse's surprise, the assembled departmental heads at Swindon agreed that it should be possible to run trains between Bristol and Bath on Sunday afternoons but there would be problems to overcome. Broad gauge trains cannot run tender first, so there would have to be a facility for turning the engine at the end of each journey. This could be done at Bristol and there was space at Bathampton to create a triangle. The job of assessing the proposal on behalf of the Swindon works was given to Alan Wild. Although an enthusiast for the idea of building the replica, Alan saw an immediate difficulty. The two-third sized wooden carriages would be unsuitable for main line running, where they would be in danger of being buffeted and even overturned by fast HSTs on the adjoining track. But he was able to point out that a somewhat larger scale could be built and still fit the tracks. Gooch had based his design in part on locomotives designed for a 5ft 6in track and the firebox was built to allow for this, so 5/6 full size would be possible. The carriages would still be on the small side but they did not have to be built strictly to the same scale as the locomotive; the vast majority of passengers would never notice the difference. If that meant the difference between running and not running a passenger service, then the purists would simply have to accept the compromise.

At this stage it all looked very feasible and the possibility of building a Firefly at Swindon was looking to be on the cards. Then there was a major reorganisation of the whole British Rail structure. The line from Bristol to Bath was now to be part of the new Intercity set up and no one was interested in running steam replicas. If the project was to go ahead, it would need totally rethinking. A new Firefly Project was set up with John Mosse as chairman and with Alan Wild playing a crucial role in the design and engineering of the replica. If recreating the original running on the Bristol-Bath route was no longer possible, then other options had to become available. If a reasonable length of old broad gauge track could be located, then a full-sized replica could be built. One area that had just such track, though not in very good condition, was on the dockside at Bristol, where there was already a thriving industrial museum. There was also an abandoned workshop with appropriate machinery that could be used for the actual work.

It was agreed that the museum and the Project would apply for a Lottery grant to provide the funding. The response was that if there were any original parts included, the funding would be available – but not if everything was to be new. In the event, not a single authenticated original component could be found. Although work was begun in the building beside the river in Bristol, it eventually had to be abandoned when it was discovered that, thanks to bank erosion, the back wall was about to disappear into the water. With no Lottery funding and nowhere to build, the Project turned to the very best available alternative. The whole operation was moved to Didcot with all the usual problems of no road access to be overcome.

Had Lottery funding been available, no doubt the whole project could have galloped ahead. As it was, things could only move on as long as there was money in the bank and volunteers available to help with the work. One very valuable fundraising scheme was the production of a set of medallions designed by John Mosse to celebrate the GWR 150th anniversary – in gold, silver and bronze. It was hoped that the gold would yield a very high profit but unfortunately production costs were far higher than expected so that never materialised, but the silver and bronze did very well. A further set was produced to mark the opening of traffic. Apart from that, most of the money was raised by individuals and a certain amount of sponsorship. With such limited financial and manpower resources available, it was decided to concentrate entirely on the locomotive and to forget about the carriages, at least for the time being.

The Didcot rebuilds had been able to reuse parts salvaged from other engines but this was not possible here. No GWR locomotives were built with 7ft wheels after the end of the broad gauge period, for example. Valve gear was still at a rather primitive stage. Forward and reverse used gab gears, which meant that there was no intermediate position between full forward and full reverse – and no way of using variable cut off for the steam. So they would have to be made – at least they were able to reuse a former signal box lever for the actual reversing lever. Although it was intended that everything should be authentic, there were limitations. Wrought iron was used for construction in the 1840s but that is virtually unobtainable today. The design of firebox and boiler would be unacceptable by modern standards – but as long as the external features were correct, no one would know what went on inside. And there were specific manufacturing problems, especially the construction of a cranked axle.

Alan Wild became Senior Planning Technician and spent two years researching and working on the details of boiler and firebox. There were original drawings available but some very specific problems to overcome. In more modern locomotives, the boiler and firebox unit is there simply to raise steam but in the earlier engine, it was an essential structural member to which, for example, the drawbar was attached. This was unacceptable, so a new arrangement had to be made – in effect to create a 'dummy' firebox that would look completely authentic, but which would hide the actual new arrangement. Alan's design was based on standard Swindon practice with a Belpaire firebox, a longitudinally welded boiler and the barrel riveted to the throat plate. The stays would be threaded for easy removal. A dummy firebox was built round the actual working component, which meant it was free to expand and contract, and it also meant that the drawbar could be firmly secured without the connection being visible from the outside. It is worth pointing out that if progress on designing the boiler seemed rather slow, there was no British standard available for welded locomotive boilers, as no new boiler of this sort had been built for half a century.

Originally, the crankaxle would have been forged as a single piece, but it was doubtful if there was anyone capable of such work today. In more modern practice, it would have been built up

Richard Antliff and his team ballasting the mixed gauge track, that allows both broad and standard gauge trains to use the system.

out of separate components, but that wasn't practical in this case. The axle was unusual in being comparatively slender but with a large throw. Welding was proposed but the idea was initially rejected by Alan Wild. An alternative proposal came from the Welding Institute – electron-beam welding. As the name suggests, this involves applying a beam of high-energy electrons to the joint, which causes the two sections to melt and flow together. Alan Wild and John Mosse were assured this would produce a very sound joint, even on such a large scale, and it should be possible to find a company with some spare time that could fit the job into a gap in their regular schedule. Then, rather to everyone's surprise, Clarke's Crank & Forge Co. of Lincoln announced that they were very happy to forge the entire axle – so the job went to them.

It was then necessary to get the designs approved by the insurers based in Manchester and John Mosse and Alan Wild made the journey north. They were told that they were rather lucky, as the assessor who saw them was about to retire and he was the last one in the company who actually had experience of engineering and was therefore able to assess a scheme so far removed from their normal line of business. But the trip turned out to be very far from lucky: along the way Mosse tripped over a paving stone and suffered a severe blow to his head. Although it didn't seem too serious at the time, within a few weeks he had died and tragically would never see the realisation of his dream.

Getting a manufacturer for the steam unit proved to be far more complex than anticipated. One of the complications was a direct result of John Mosse's death. He had combined the duties of chair and treasurer, but now the roles were split between Dr Sam Bee as chair and Roger Langley as treasurer. The latter decided that it was inappropriate to have a member of the Trust having responsibility for design since, if things went wrong, the Trust would have to bear the full responsibility. So a new design was commissioned and new quotes obtained. The job finally went to Isaac Newton & Co and Alan Wild was pleased to discover that many of his design features were incorporated in the finished product.

Firefly differed from the *Iron Duke* replica in many ways, other than basic design. For example, the front buffer on the latter was purely cosmetic, while that on *Firefly* was a six-inch thick baulk of seasoned oak. Over the years, the different components had to be manufactured, including the wheels. It appears that originally, the construction of the wheels proceeded much as they would have done if they had been wooden wheels made by a wheelwright. Individually forged spokes were fitted into the rim – which must have been an extraordinarily complex operation. For the replica, casting was the obvious first choice.

The project took far longer than perhaps anyone had ever envisaged when the idea was first put forward in the 1980s but in 2005, the almost completed locomotive was moved from the engine shed to the transfer shed – though the tall chimney had to be removed – when the engine shed was constructed no one was expecting it to accommodate a locomotive with a chimney top 14ft 10in above the rails. The tender soon followed and at last it was possible to carry out test steaming of the broad gauge engine on broad gauge tracks. That year, the locomotive was finally unveiled. By this time, a broad gauge third class carriage had also been completed and could be united with its engine. With the Firefly Project completed, the finished replica was handed over to the Society and is now a permanent part of the collection.

The Firefly project had been a great success and added immeasurably to the recreation of the broad gauge years. Another interesting piece of equipment was purchased for the Society by the Bristol Group in 2008. It was really little more than a piece of serendipity that it arrived there. Some members were visiting the Royal Navy Dockyard at Devonport and were told there was something that might interest them – and it was destined either to be sold at a modest price or scrapped. This was a 38ft diameter broad gauge turntable that was probably installed at the dockyard in 1868. The Cornwall Railway were providing a short loop beside the basin in North Dock. The turntable was ordered from Heanett & Spinks and it is generally thought that this was that turntable, even though it had subsequently been moved to the South Yard. Because they have quite a small diameter, turntables such as this are generally known as 'wagon turntables'. It is now installed near the entrance to the site. Visitors who stop to inspect it might wonder about the mechanism that was used to move it. The answer is – there wasn't any. The wagon or small locomotive was wheeled onto the turntable, and then pushed round manually.

Originally, it had been hoped to include it in a museum at the dockyard, but that never happened and Devonport's loss was Didcot's gain. Agreeing to purchase a turntable at a mutually acceptable price was the simple part. Documentation was needed and officialdom moved with deadly slowness. This would not,

The break of gauge at Gloucester meant that everything had to be transferred from one train system to the other – a nuisance that eventually led to the demise of the broad gauge. Didcot volunteers are re-enacting the chaotic scene.

of course, have surprised Mr Brunel, who once described the Admiralty as having 'an unlimited supply of some negative principle which seems to absorb and eliminate everything that approaches them'. Eventually, permission was granted for the turntable to be removed and contractors appointed, but then at the very last moment it was discovered that one vital document had not been issued. Fortunately, the head of security was quite happy to accept the written acknowledgement that the agreed cheque had indeed been issued and received and he ordered the gate to be opened to allow the material to leave. That, of course, is only part of the story. What arrived at Didcot was a mass of cast iron – not material to deal with carelessly, for unlike wrought iron or steel it is brittle. There were also a large number of large granite blocks. All this had to be manhandled into place and reset in its present position near the entrance.

Another relic from the early days when Brunel was the man in charge is a pipe from the famous – or infamous – atmospheric railway. Various notions had been put forward at the start of the nineteenth century for utilising the fact that if you create a vacuum on one side of a piston enclosed in a tube, then air pressure on the opposite side will force the piston to move. This was not exactly new – it was after all the principal applied by Thomas Newcomen when he built his pioneering beam engines. What was new was the idea that the pipe should be long enough to provide power for a railway train. The first, wildly impractical notion was to make the carriage the piston and drive the whole thing along a tube. Persuading passengers to use such a device might have proved troublesome, even if it could be made to work. Eventually a more practical idea emerged in 'Mr. Clegg's Pneumatic Railway' on a short line in London. In this version, an iron pipe was laid with a slot along the top, through which a projection on the piston could travel. In order to maintain the vacuum, the whole length of the slit was covered by a leather and iron flap, which would open to allow the piston to pass and close behind it. This was actually put to use in the Dublin & Kingston Railway. And the idea attracted many engineers to come and investigate. George Stephenson declared it to be 'humbug' but Brunel was impressed. He decided to use it for the Great Western extension, west of Exeter. The first trial section between Exeter and Teignmouth was opened in 1846. Steam engines had been installed along the route to create the vacuum – one of these engine houses is still preserved at Dawlish. The scheme was not a success. Evacuating the pipes took far longer than Brunel had anticipated, and there were long delays as trains waited to move from one section to the next. A far greater problem occurred when winter arrived. The leather valve froze and became stiff and virtually useless. Worse was to follow; the leather soon began to deteriorate and rot due to chemical reactions. The scheme was abandoned in favour of a conventional steam railway. The pipe at Didcot may not look to be the most fascinating item on display, but it is a reminder that even genius is fallible. It represents one of Brunel's greatest errors of judgement.

One of the problems all railway companies faced in the early years was traffic control. It was essential that drivers knew that it was safe to proceed or be told it was essential to stop. So, signals were required. Inevitably, the Great Western developed its own unique system, which will be described in more detail in the chapter on signalling.

CHAPTER SEVEN

Site Development

A casual visitor to Didcot will enjoy seeing the locomotives and rolling stock, visiting the museum and perhaps having a bite to eat in the café or browsing the books and souvenirs in the shop. What they will not perhaps be aware of is the huge amount of work that has gone into the things they take for granted. Many of the buildings they visit were not there when the Society first moved onto the site; the walkways that make access easy and safe did not exist. That they do exist today is largely due to the volunteers who do the very unglamorous jobs on site. Visitors may envy the volunteers who get to work on the footplate – they are less likely to envy the many who might be asked get up early in the morning to do jobs such as mixing concrete. But without them we would not have the Didcot Centre we know today.

When the Society first arrived at Didcot, the site was very much one of working buildings. The main structures were the engine

A typical scene at Didcot when the Society first arrived and it was still being used by British Rail.

shed with the lifting shop immediately behind it and the coal stage. The engine shed, constructed in 1932, is a rare survivor from the age of steam, which still has all but one of its wooden smoke hoods in the roof, which kept the building ventilated when locomotives were in steam. The workshop behind it was used for lifting boilers. Engine sheds had been standardised in the Churchward era, all built as straight line sheds, mostly having a repair shop attached and a turntable immediately outside the front of the shed. This is a building with a social as well as a technological history. In the years after the First World War, when unemployment was a catastrophic problem, the government passed a Loan and Guarantee Act in 1929, which provided money for companies looking to expand. The GWR was badly in need of more depots to service the fleet and built nine new depots, of which one was Didcot.

The coal stage actually has two functions. At the top is a cast iron water tank that fed down to the water crane that was used to fill locomotive boilers. Beneath that is the coal store, approached by a ramp. This allows coal trucks to be brought up to the top for unloading and from the store the coal can be dropped down into locomotive tenders. These are essentially practical, utilitarian structures – still being used as they were when first constructed, though water is now supplied from a water tower originally installed at Bodmin. They are also quite rare survivors from the steam age, which is why they are both listed structures that have to be preserved by law. There were two other structures on site, one of which was the ash shed. This was a rather flimsy structure, added during the Second World War, so that engines could drop their fire under cover and the glow from the hot ashes would not be visible from the air. Didcot, in fact, escaped more or less unscathed from the war years. At the time, however, air raids were an ever-present threat and the company built air raid shelters for the staff, one of which has been restored and is now open to the public.

The essentials were there for a rail centre of sorts, but there were many more facilities that the site would need to develop, both to make it more accessible to the general public, but also to be more fully representative of every aspect of life on the Great Western. But if you are based on a historic site and want to expand its facilities, you cannot just put up any old building and hope that it will somehow fit in and function well. Richard Antliff, the civil engineering manager, has a very clear view of what is needed. The first priority is to develop a deep understanding of Great Western practice and

The coal stage had a double function: providing water from the tank on top and coal from the bunker underneath. Locomotive 3650 has just climbed the ramp – in working days it would have hauled coal trucks to replenish the bunker.

style, which involves studying old photos and visiting existing sites. Research shows sites that were neat and tidy and generally quite unfussy. There is a fundamental difference between depots and stations. The latter were designed to attract customers and could be quite flamboyant; the original Temple Meads station with its mock medieval hammer beam roof is one outstanding example while at the other end of the line, Paddington has quite rightly often been referred to as a Cathedral of Steam. Depots have no need of such fripperies as the public rarely set foot in them. But that does not mean that they are ugly – like many buildings designed for function, they can have their own austere character. To understand them, one has to look at the materials used – brick, stone, iron and steel and how they were employed. Colour schemes give unity to different buildings and all these factors have to be taken into account when adding new structures to the old site. The use of materials is crucial – a plastic façade would be a disaster in such a situation. So new buildings must always be designed to sit comfortably with the old.

In many parts of the site, instead of building new structures, old Great Western buildings were acquired and reused. The first thing visitors see is the ticket office at the entrance that is itself a good example of adaptation. The main building started life as a simple hut for the ground frame at Didcot station, but it has been enlarged by the addition of a porch. The two marry up so well that they look as if they have always been together. Rural branch lines, such as that between Newbury and Lambourn, often had a succession of small halts, which did not justify the expense of creating grand stations. But passengers needed somewhere to wait in bad weather, so they were supplied with modest shelters built from corrugated iron. But even these had a slightly exotic appearance, being topped with a curved, pagoda style roof. One of these from the Lambourn line now stands at what is now Didcot Halt on the Society's own short branch line. It was removed from the Stockcross and Bagnor Hall Halt and re-erected here in 1977.

Removing old buildings, bringing them onto site and then reconstructing them was never an easy task, but it represented a great saving in money over a new build – and gave the site authentic Great Western buildings that have that special patina that comes with age and long service. But it was impossible to fulfil every requirement in this way. There were some projects where there was no choice; money had to be acquired for materials and labour to build entirely new structures. The first really big project came about from the urgent need to find somewhere to keep and preserve the rapidly growing and increasingly rare and valuable collection of coaches. It would have to be a new build and would be expensive, so a special fundraising exercise was begun in 1976. Initial results were quite disappointing. The Newsletter of October that year recorded the sad fact that of the £15,000 needed, only £6,000 had been raised and only around 500 of the 3,000 members had so far chipped in. Nevertheless, the cover for the coaches was so badly needed that it was decided to go ahead with the contract for the foundations and to get tenders for the construction, even if it meant taking out loans.

On most projects of this kind, the start would be quite simple; the contractors would turn up with everything they needed for the job and get down to work. But the situation at Didcot is not like that; there is no road access. That means that everything had to be brought in by rail. That creates a bit of a problem when you've got a 450 ton train arriving that needs shunting and all you have is a 200 horse power diesel to do the job. The answer was simply to split the train in two and move the two halves separately. Then it was

One of the first open days at Didcot, with some locomotives on static display and others in steam.

possible to unload the impressive array of equipment that included a dumper truck, a JCB and a machine for excavating and levelling the ground. The latter was to prove very useful while it was on site in preparing the ground for laying new track. But the immediate job in hand was preparing the foundations for the new building, which would include not just a shed for holding the exhibits but also a workshop for restoration and repair work. Much of the site was not covered in firm soil but by ash, released from locomotives for many decades. This was not an ideal foundation, so a special system was introduced that had been developed in the Netherlands, where a lot of building work had to be carried out on loose, sandy soil. This used hollow reinforced concrete posts held together by a steel mesh. But before that could start, the ground had to be cleared and levelled, a job that was described in a Newsletter at the time as involving 'the expenditure of much blood and sweat'. Needless to say, the blood, sweat and perhaps a few tears came from the volunteer workers.

When it came to erecting the steel frame early in 1977, the Society's own equipment came into its own. The steam crane was used and for a machine that had effectively been pensioned off years ago, it worked remarkably well. In just 10 days, the whole frame was in place and ready for cladding. Once completed, the new building sat very comfortably with its older neighbouring engine shed. This set the pattern for a great deal of the development work that was to follow over the decades. Careful plans were made and costed, then

Advertising the 1970 Open Day.

the money had to be raised. Wherever possible, work would be done by volunteers, but certain jobs had to be left to the contractors. In making the estimates, it was always kept in mind that materials that were used had to be appropriate for a historic site and the need to preserve authenticity. That often meant having to buy bespoke material rather than cheaper off the shelf alternatives. Visitors might not appreciate this when they visit – but they would certainly notice if it hadn't been done. If, for example, no one sees any obvious difference between the engine shed and the carriage shed then that shows the scheme has been entirely successful in achieving its aims of authenticity.

Although it had been essential to prioritise providing a new building to prevent the deterioration of the coaching stock, by the early '80s, the site itself had become something of a mess. This was highlighted in 1979 by the editor of the *Railway Magazine*, who described visitors picking their way through all kinds of debris. That is not the sort of publicity any society wants to attract, so a clean-up was immediately put in hand. In particular, the engine shed was given a thorough going over and the result was a building in which it was possible to walk around without either getting dirty clothes or tripping over obstacles. Criticism may not always be welcomed, but it can be a valuable spur to action – and the response was entirely appropriate. This whole business of making the site both attractive and welcoming was continued in ways that visitors may not even notice. It has to be remembered that this site was once deep in ash – and anyone walking around for very long with white socks would end the day with black hosiery. Now there is a firm concrete pathway from the entrance and wooden walkways crossing the tracks. They make visits far more comfortable and, even more importantly, safer. Creating this system was just another of those tasks that require a lot of very hard work but get very little public praise. Improvements extended to landscaping the site, building attractive boundary fences, providing appropriate seating and a whole variety of small things that add together to make the experience of a visit to Didcot a pleasant one.

One of the most important projects was the creation of a satisfactory running line – now known as the main line. This was not something that happened overnight. More land was acquired in the 1980s and the Society took on the job of laying the track. They designed their own way of doing things. They had a wagon to hold the sleepers, which could then be pulled out of the front and set in place. Short rails were then added, to enable the wagon to move forward. The short rails would then be replaced by standard rails, once a sufficient number of sleepers were down. British Rail were to do the tamping, but the volunteers undertook the ballasting. 340 tons of ballast was brought on site in 4-wheeled hoppers. Richard Antliff was the man in charge and he discovered that no one else had any experience of the work. So he had to issue instructions to the workforce. One of the main points he made was that the signal to stop was to raise both hands in the air but he warned this should only be used if there was real danger of a serious accident. The hopper would stop immediately, but the load wouldn't. So the volunteers would find a huge heap of stone that would have to be shovelled up by hand. In the event, all went well. With track in position, there was also a need for suitable platforms at either end of the route.

The northern end was named 'Oxford Road', even though it is a long way from that city. It does, however, follow a long GWR tradition of naming stations as 'Something Road', when they were

Removing the ground frame shed from Didcot station that has now been reconstituted as the ticket office at the entrance to the site.

actually a long way from the place they were serving. Wantage Road is, of course, the classic example, where the station was so far from the town they had to build the tramway to join them. Work on site is never hurried. The Society very rarely applies for grants for this sort of work, simply because – apart from the vast amount of paperwork generated in the applications – any money that is raised usually comes with a strict timetable. GWS is run by and for amateurs who want to enjoy the experience and not be pressurised by deadlines. There is also the very practical consideration that if things have to be done in too much of a hurry, they tend to go wrong. It is always cheaper to avoid mistakes than correct them later. So the job of building up the platform wall went on through the '90s. The coping stones are authentic having been originally used at Tiverton Junction. Getting them loaded up was complicated by the fact that the work had to be carried out close to a working line, so the Society had to have the co-operation of British Rail and post lookouts. More stone was acquired than needed for the job in hand but nothing is wasted. There is now a stock available for other jobs and for any necessary repairs. The stone slabs were laid using an improvised crane constructed out of bridge rail, which worked perfectly well, and the platform was tarmacked and ready to greet the new millennium. At the opposite end, the platform was created out of prefabricated concrete

The assembled frame for what would become the new carriage shed.

sections, based on a design used at Eynsham. The waiting room is a replica of a typical GWR structure at a small station or halt.

Every building that was erected on site needed the same careful planning and so did the general layout of the site. It was clear that with so much going on over the years that there needed to be someone in charge of the civil engineering side of things. Richard Antliff had already been busy on various projects for the Society and had always believed in the clear advantage of having good drawings in the early stages. Once these have been approved, there is less chance of things going wrong during construction. In the early '90s, the Society bought the redundant Heyford Station from British Rail. Richard Antliff had a vision of how it might be used; as he said, he could envisage how visitors would approach the road side, how they would be greeted by the ticking of a clock in the booking hall and how a small goods yard could be created with a hand crane in place. He presented the whole scheme to a management council meeting, rolling out his 13-foot-long drawing to explain his ideas. At the time, there was little chance of funds being available to realise the idea, but Graham Perry was so impressed that he suggested Richard should be appointed as development manager. He accepted the idea and over the next

Work under way installing the traverser in front of the carriage shed that helps in the movement of rolling stock out onto the running lines.

few years he would be producing many more of his detailed drawings. Heyford Station, however, remains an unrealised dream, but many other projects went forward

New buildings continued to be erected, including a special shed to house the steam railmotor. As far as is known there were only ever two designated sheds specifically built for railcars – one at Southall on the main line from Paddington and the other at Chalford on the Cheltenham line near Stroud. The latter is not even a halt today, but it does have one unusual feature that is worth mentioning. When the line was built, it cut off a woollen mill and mill house from the road, so the Great Western agreed to supply a manned level crossing in perpetuity – and it is still there and still manned. The Chalford shed actually burned down in 1916, taking railcar No 42 with it. The decision was taken to base the Didcot shed as closely as possible on the Southall version. This was 200ft long and 19ft wide, constructed with an iron frame with corrugated iron sides – which at least ensured it didn't suffer the fate of wooden framed Chalford. The roof was curved with a smoke trough running the length of the curved roof and a pit down the centre of the floor. When first built in 1906, the smoke vented through chimneys that were notably ineffective, so that maintenance in the building was rather like working in a perpetual fog. This was later

The official inauguration of the turntable that was originally installed at Southampton.

improved by fitting louvered vents running the length of the roof. This was the model used by Richard Antliff, who designed the shed for Didcot. Work began in January 2006 on preparing the site, while Peter Jennings and a team of volunteers started laying track towards the shed, using both a steam and diesel crane. Everything seemed set for a very successful venture when Network Rail made an astonishing announcement; they withdrew their offer to sell the site. This might have been accepted as a disastrous end to the whole project but Society members do not give in that easily. It was decided to go ahead with the preparatory work while intensive negotiations went on to persuade Network Rail to reverse their decision. It took until December 2009 but at last permission was given for the land to be acquired and the shed to be built. It was a triumph for optimism and perseverance and work went ahead on the new building. It was completed in 2010, with a small annexe at the side to tell the history of the railcar.

The biggest change came when the Society acquired an extra slice of land and there was an opportunity to advance some of the schemes that had been put on hold because of lack of space. The process was so slow because Network Rail were unwilling to part with the land in case they needed it for some unspecified purpose in the future and negotiations dragged on for around twenty years. But at least that provided plenty of time for long term planning. A programme was begun known as Far Horizons that looked at all the projects that would be possible in an ideal world. Some forty suggestions were made and discussed and then whittled down to a more manageable ten top priorities. These included a much bigger museum for small artefacts and an archive, more storage for rolling stock, some of which were still out in the open and subject to deterioration, and a decent restaurant area. With the new land available, some at least were to be put into effect.

Plans were drawn up that would include all kinds of desirable structures including a large exhibition hall and drawings were produced, showing how the new buildings would continue to represent traditional railway practices. Some of these buildings have now been completed, including the improved refreshment area and new museum block. There is now a well laid out visitor area that includes the café, the shop and those unromantic but essential edifices – the Ladies and Gents. Contractors were brought in, but they were working under the careful supervision of Richard Antliff on behalf of the Society to ensure everything was done to

Richard Antliff's drawing to show the layout and details for what would become the broad gauge section.

the very highest standards. Sometimes schemes take an unexpected twist. Some time had been spent on building an electric switch room with a transformer next door that was originally planned as a workshop. Then the Swindon Panel Society approached Didcot to say they had acquired the electric switch board – a 28ft long panel for signal control. It was too good an opportunity to miss. In the early days, the GWS had the opportunity to acquire the Exeter West signal box with all its signalling equipment, but it was beyond their resources at the time. Now there is a certain amount of regret that the opportunity was not grabbed, though at least the Exeter box was not scrapped but found a new home at the Crewe Heritage Centre. Even so, there is a feeling that it is a little unfortunate that this grand structure left the Great Western empire for foreign parts. So although the Swindon panel is more modern than anything else on site, it has been brought to Didcot and this has involved considerable changes to the building. The workshop will now become a train management exhibition.

Two buildings are not directly concerned with the displays – the restaurant and the shop – but are important parts of the whole organisation. In the very early days, when the site was only open to visitors on Bank Holidays, catering for visitors only took place in part of one of the sheds. As numbers increased, a kitchen and café were constructed. The volunteer workers got served their food from the door at the back of the kitchen and then had to go and find somewhere to sit down and eat it. But as numbers increased this became less acceptable, so today there is a proper staff canteen next to the kitchen. This was not the only catering offered by the Society. Wine and dine evenings in dining cars proved a great attraction and brought visitors to Didcot, who were not necessarily train enthusiasts as such but enjoyed the experience. For a long time, all this activity depended entirely on volunteers. In 1983, Jeanette Howse was appointed as a full time administrator and catering came under her remit. In fact it is fair to say that it virtually took over her life. She worked in the office all week and her work included ordering food and supervising its delivery on top of other duties, while at weekends she worked in the restaurant itself. Eventually, it became clear that it was all too much for volunteers to cope with, no matter how enthusiastic, for visitor numbers were growing all the time, reaching a peak of around 150,000 a year. The first thought was to bring in an outside catering firm to run things, but this was not a success and the Society soon decided it was time to employ its own caterers as it still does today. Jeanette, relieved of her weekend catering, said she sat in her garden on a Saturday afternoon and thought to herself – 'What do I do?' Didcot had become her life. She soon found other activities to keep her busy.

Starting the process of laying broad gauge track in the Brunel manner, with the rails on longitudinal sleepers, held together by metal ties.

She made jam from produce grown on site for sale and encouraged other ladies to come and join her – more visitors for the centre.

All museums and visitor attractions know the value of a good shop. They provide a service for visitors – and make money for the Society. Rather like the catering, in the early days it was a little ramshackle. The first shop was little better than a garden shed, just about able to hold two people at a time. There was a door to get into it, and an unglazed opening on the opposite wall, covered by a wooden shutter. Once that was removed, customers could be served through the gap. The chance to get something better came as a result of improvements elsewhere on the site. When the concrete path was laid from the ticket office, the site office was a Portakabin. When work was completed, it became the new shop. The shed was then taken over by the Freight group's sales team, who were raising money for the restoration of the 2-8-0 Collett, number 3822. They sold a variety of goods including t-shirts with appropriate themes, including the memorable message 'Brunel Rules IK'. Eventually, it was decided that it was time to have a proper building, and once that was completed it became another of Jeanette's projects to turn the running of the shop into a more professional operation. This meant a complete refurbishment, installing purpose-built racks and shelves – largely done by Mark from the carriage department. Second-hand units were also bought, one of which started life in a very different environment – as a showcase for ladies' underwear. Eventually the work was completed and the stock room shelved, but it was not quite the end of the story. The flat roof did what flat roofs so often do – it leaked. It was replaced by the present hipped roof. The shop too is now overseen by a professional manager. Shop and restaurant are valuable sources of income. Although it has never required a separate building, another vital part of the administration's work, and a very profitable one, is providing facilities for filming – everything from pop videos to feature films.

There was one major problem affecting the whole of the site development programme as the twentieth century came to an end. The lease on the site was due to expire in 2019 and there seemed to be a reluctance to get down to any serious negotiations over its renewal. The Society had the two major listed buildings, the engine shed and the coaling stage, to maintain but lacked the funds to do the job properly. They were unable to apply for any grants simply because there was no guarantee they would still be able to use the site when the existing lease came to an end. It was all

very frustrating – and although it was a matter of urgency for the
Society, it was very low on the list of priorities for Network Rail.
A meeting was finally held in November 2009 with the local MP, Ed
Vaizey, present. It began with Network Rail explaining the different
schemes that had been put forward by Great Western for the site,
which included a flyover and two new platforms, both of which
had been rejected as uneconomic. But there were still objections
from the engineering department to any renewal of the lease –
though no one had actually come up with any suggestion as to why
they might need it. A possibility of a 35-year lease was put forward,
with a proviso that if the land was needed, compensation would be
paid for any investment by the Society. It was a shorter lease than
the Society wanted and there were obviously a lot of problems that
still needed to be overcome and negotiations dragged on. Help
came from an unexpected meeting. John Scott Morgan, a member of
the Society since 1967, had been asked to substitute for a colleague
at an important social event to represent the company he worked
for. Among the guests was the Transport Minister Lord Adonis.
So John plucked up his courage and went to speak to him about
the situation at Didcot. The Minister, it turned out, knew all about
Didcot, was sympathetic and simply asked to have all the facts sent

The new tracks
leading away from
the transit shed,
home to the two
broad gauge
replicas.

to him. He even collared John at the end of the function to stress his willingness to help. John phoned Richard Croucher at 11 pm to pass on the message that he needed to send the detail to the Transport Minister the next day. As a result, real progress was finally being made and by 2011 the Society had been offered a fifty-year lease.

This ended a period of nerve-racking uncertainty and made it possible to plan for the future. Among the many ideas being discussed are an improvement in the educational facility. Liaison with local schools and ensuring that visits are meaningful for the students and chime in with curriculum requirements are vital parts of the work of the Society. Many would like to improve the restaurant facilities, so that Didcot becomes a place where people actually want to come for a meal in pleasant surroundings. And there are some who believe that as those who actually remember the age of steam inevitably dwindle, the Society should look beyond the golden years of the GWR to a later period. Will vintage diesels ever have the appeal of the older locomotives? That is certainly a question for discussion and not without controversy. One thing is certain; the site will continue to develop and new projects will be started. And what is equally certain is that there will always be plenty of hard work for willing volunteers to do.

The Centre as visitors first see it today; they may not appreciate it, but the walkway laid by the volunteers has saved them trudging through layers of compacted ash.

CHAPTER EIGHT

The Museum

From quite an early period in the Society's history, opportunities arose for acquiring small objects but what was lacking was a place to store them, apart from the attics and sheds of members who could be persuaded to make space for them. But there is no point in acquiring objects unless they can be accessed and displayed. Apart from objects, the Society also began to acquire some interesting documents of historical significance. Once again, the problem arose of how to conserve them and make them available to anyone seriously interested in the history of the Great Western Railway. In the early stages, the London group offered to look after the paper archive, with the idea that one day they might form the basis for a useful reference library. Other items such as uniforms and various bits of hardware found a home wherever space was available in Didcot. All collections, however, have to have a starting point.

Fred Gray was one of the enthusiastic volunteers who came to Didcot and he took control of the group building the ticket office and the Didcot Halt platform. When he saw another volunteer putting a piece of hardware in a container, it seemed to him that objects such as this were every bit as important in telling the story of the Great Western as were the more obvious locomotives and rolling stock. He began collecting the disparate items together, restoring them when necessary and then arranged for them to be shown to the public. There was no museum building at this stage but there was a corridor carriage available. Items were arranged within the different compartments, which became temporary display cases, and the general public could walk down the corridor to view them. The experiment was a success. As a result, it was agreed that artefacts and documents needed their own permanent home. A railway carriage was inadequate – a new building would be needed and work went ahead on the construction as part of the complex along with the shop and restaurant.

The Small Relics Display opened to the public for the first time in August 1982, but it was always regarded as a temporary measure. The crucial event in ensuring that these items should be properly treated came when Ron King Bird decided that the Society should

The Antiquary – unwanted small objects being sold off.

eventually receive his vast collection of paperwork relating to all aspects of GWR life. Such a large and important bequest encouraged others to think of the GWS as likely custodians for their collections and artefacts. It was decided that with the amount of material that was now being amassed, then there should be a new Trust set up specifically to care for it. The result was the formation of the Great Western Trust in 1984, a registered charity, with seven trustees, all GWS volunteers. None were professional curators but what they lacked in curatorial experience they made up for by enthusiasm to learn. There was a great deal of work to be done.

If one is serious about preserving artefacts and archive material then you have to go for ideal conservation practices, which means providing a secure environment in which temperature and humidity can be carefully controlled. And that costs a great deal of money. Thirty years after the museum opened, it was finally announced that work on an annexe – the Charles Gordon Stuart Annexe – to house a library and museum store was about to get under way. It was estimated that the foundations could be laid for £20,000 and that a further £150,000 would be needed for completion of the building itself. There was enough money to start work on the foundations and it was hoped that actually seeing work get under way would be an inspiration and money would be raised. The design, as with everything at Didcot, echoes GWR practice. It is built of the same brick as the original Small Relics Display building, but with a higher pitched roof, at the same angle as the Churchward engine shed at Old Oak Common, and is graced with a little clock tower based on one also at Old Oak, on the Carriage and Wagon offices.

The actual construction was carried out by contractors brought in and supervised by Richard Antliff and gradually the new building was brought into use. In the summer of 2014, the job of transferring items from the various sheds in which they had been stored into the new building got under way. Immediately behind the actual museum is the library and reading room, supplied with entirely appropriate furniture; the large table originally stood in the Ladies Room at Reading Signal Works and the chairs came from a variety of Great Western offices. Bookshelves line the walls and are themselves filled with books and journals dealing with all aspects of GWR history. These are available for study by appointment but most of those who come here are far more interested in the original documents stored in the rest of the annexe. This area contains a vast amount of material – far more than could ever be put on display in the exhibition space. So why store so much if it cannot be seen by the public? There are two very good reasons. The first is that

The new museum and archive building.

The Archive
reading room.

many visitors make repeat visits to Didcot and there is a very good case to be made for changing the exhibits every now and then, so that there is always something new to see. The other reason is that the items preserved here are all worth preserving. No one knows what the future holds and it may be that in time there will be an opportunity to expand the display area, even if there are no plans to do so at present. These are items that are going to be available when and if needed – and a lot of material is also a valuable resource for researchers. It is simply prudent to keep anything that should be preserved – and conserve it to the very highest standard.

The annexe is not large, so every effort has to be made to utilise the space to the full. Roll out mesh frames are the ideal space savers. They are easily moved by turning a wheel, which means that instead of having aisles between each frame, there is only the one aisle created by moving the frames until there is space to access the one needed. An important part of this system contains the racks holding the framed posters, which cover an immense range in time, style and subject matter. The actual design of the frames was the work of a Trustee, Paddy Baker. The very important paper archive is housed in conservation grade storage boxes, and each individual item is in a transparent sleeve. This means that all items can be looked at without handling and damaging the original. The many other items are all treated with equal respect. This may not be an area that most of the public sees but it is absolutely vital to the preservation of so much priceless material.

Walking into the public area of the museum the first impression is of a rather old-fashioned display – and that is intended as a compliment. There has been a tendency in some quarters to make the act of displaying more important than the object displayed. Walk into many museums and you are faced with a battery of flickering screens, distracting the eye from the exhibits themselves. This allegedly appeals to a younger generation brought up on modern technology. The trouble with that argument is that in many museums the technology rather than being 'modern' looks sadly dated. Teenagers can usually get better graphics on their phones. One of my own grandsons when in his young teens complained bitterly about the 'improvements' that had been made to a local museum; the displays all looked very elegant, but he had lost the fun of pulling open drawers and finding things for himself. The Didcot museum really invites you to look at objects and find the stories behind them. It is a reminder that railways are far more than just a means of transport; they have transformed the social life of the country in all kinds of different ways. The museum reflects the rich variety of railway life.

In an earlier age, the railway dining car was a sumptuous affair, where you were served food on fine starched linen, on plates adorned with the railway crest and silver cutlery. And, of course, wines were poured into cut glass drinking vessels. The same standards were carried over to the railway hotels. There is a small display helping to recreate that experience, and in among the cutlery it would be easy to overlook a pair of grapefruit spoons. They are something of a rarity in most households these days, but they were very practical items – with a cutting edge on one side to slice through the tougher fibres. But there is also a story behind these simple items. A couple sent them to Didcot and were rather embarrassed at having to tell how they acquired them. It seems that many years ago, they spent their honeymoon in the GWR Tregenna Castle Hotel and lifted them as souvenirs. They had never really dared use them but they felt they could finally salve their consciences by presenting them to the museum.

One of the joys of this museum is that every item seems to have its own intriguing story – even the most commonplace. Who, for

One of the oldest GWR posters in the collection, dating back to Edwardian days.

GREAT WESTERN RAILWAY.

WESTON SUPER MARE

GRAND PIER & PAVILION

KÄNDT'S FAMOUS BAND AND HIGH CLASS ENTERTAINMENTS DAILY.

CHEAP EXCURSIONS

to Weston-super-Mare

DURING THE SUMMER MONTHS.

FOR

WEEKLY FROM PADDINGTON STATION.

HALF-DAY, DAY, OR Longer Periods.

AT FREQUENT INTERVALS FROM MANY Provincial Towns.

TOURIST TICKETS

from LONDON and many Provincial Towns.

WEEK-END TICKETS.

Full Particulars of Train Service, SPECIAL CHEAP FACILITIES, etc., etc., obtainable at the Company's Stations and Offices.

THE MENDIP PRESS, LTD., "GAZETTE" WORKS, WESTON-SUPER-MARE. E.S.& A.Robinson Lt Bristol.

example, could get excited about a pair of blankets, even if one of them still has its GWR insignia still embroidered on it? But these blankets have a dramatic history. Among the fleet of small ships that went to rescue the British troops waiting on the beaches at Dunkirk in the Second World War were GWR steamers. When the men were pulled wet and shivering from the water they were wrapped in blankets. One soldier at least never returned his – and the relatives kept them over the years until one day they decided that if they couldn't be returned to the GWR they should at least find a home in the GWR museum.

Grapefruit spoons and blankets can seem insignificant and can easily be overlooked. The same could not be said of one of the most spectacular exhibits that occupies a prominent position at the far end of the room. In May 2013, there was an article in the Society's magazine, the *Great Western Echo*, about Engine No 1 designed by William Dean, chief engineer at Swindon from 1877 to 1902. The engine was a 4-4-0T built in 1880 that ran until 1924. Michael Dean, a direct descendant of the famous engineer, spent seventeen years building a working replica of this locomotive to run on a 5-inch gauge track. He read the article in the magazine and most generously offered his model to the museum. It is a thing of beauty, immaculate in its detailing and well deserves its place of honour. It is above all a monument to the patience and skill of the model maker.

Most of the exhibits are concerned with the world of work, the running of the railway and attracting customers. But there are also reminders that the company had an enormous staff, particularly in Swindon, and that their social lives were often bound up with the company as well as the working life. There is a programme for the Operatic Society's performance of *A Country Girl*, a comic opera in two acts, with music by Lionel Monckton, which has now been more or less forgotten. But when it opened in the West End in 1902, it ran for 728 performances. It was apparently very popular with amateurs and looking through the list of musical numbers, it is difficult to get an idea of what it was like. One song had the intriguing beginning: 'Oh Molly was tall and fair to see, her manners were frank, her language free'. One wonders which young Swindon worker got that saucy part in 1939. And there would have been no shortage of musicians for, like many big works at that time, Swindon had its own band.

The Didcot Centre mainly concentrates on vehicles running on rails, but the museum has reminders that this was by no means the only transport system used by the GWR. They had their own delivery vans, at first drawn by horses and then replaced by motors. They had a regular steamer service that carried passengers to Ireland, the Channel Islands and France – but not following the great engineer's plans of crossing the Atlantic to America. A ship's wheel is just one of the items to remind us of those days. In 1933, the company took to the air, forming GWR Air Service with just one plane. It was a short-lived venture; the following year it joined the other major companies that formed the Big Four to create Railway Air Services. Many of the passengers were carried in that famous workhorse of the air, the de Havilland Rapide, a model of which is on display. Like all the best exhibits these provide a tantalising glimpse into parts of history that might otherwise be ignored.

Walking round the collection various displays grab one's attention. There are reminders of the fact that the GWR was always keen to attract customers by advertising destinations through their posters; the Society has a magnificent collection, far more in store

A sophisticated poster from the 1930s.

SPEED TO THE WEST
CORNWALL DEVON SOMERSET WALES

than can be displayed at any one time. But the posters are also a reminder of how tastes change. It is difficult to imagine any railway company these days advertising all the spa towns that could be visited. And the rail enthusiasts are not forgotten – there is a display of old locomotive guides, treasured by so many train spotters down the years. And a model rail set up with old tinplate stations and figures takes older visitors back to childhood days. Then there are the oddities, like a notice from Swindon informing workers that jumping over engine pits was forbidden. On a more sombre note, there is a section on wartime activities; Swindon built a hospital train for the First World War that was paid for by UK Flour Millers Company. And of course, there are name and number plates galore. It is fair to say that there is no aspect of the company's history that isn't represented in some form or other.

It is impossible to describe everything in the collection, either on display or in store, but the curator Peter Rance and I chose a few examples for their intrinsic interest, the stories they had to tell and to give an idea of the range of material. Two very different items have a close geographical connection. On 13 June 1842, Queen Victoria made the first ever rail journey by a British monarch. She had been staying at Windsor but had to make her way to the nearest station, Slough, for the trip to Paddington. It was a momentous occasion with both Brunel and Daniel Gooch on the footplate. It was to be the first of many royal train journeys and she travelled in a suitably grand royal coach. But the company wanted to make quite sure that the event was obvious to anyone who happened to see the passing train and so a special headlamp was produced, topped by an imposing crown. It is on display at Didcot.

When the original Bill was presented to Parliament, it contained provision for a station at Windsor, serving that town and Eton across the water. But the Provost of Eton College objected on the grounds that the arrival of the railway would undermine the morality of the boys who could take advantage of it to savour the evils of London life. When the Bill went to Parliament, the proposed line was rejected – hardly surprising given the number of Old Etonians in the Commons and the Lords. In the twenty-first century, the Society bought an early railway map at an auction, showing part of the line. It was only after it was acquired that it was realised that it showed a line to Windsor and Eton, so this map must have been one of the originals prepared when the Bill was brought to Parliament. It is perhaps fair to say that if the other bidders had realised its significance it would have cost a great deal more – and could well have ended up in a private collection. Instead, Didcot is now in possession of a fascinating piece of GWR history.

The special lamp that was placed on royal trains when Queen Victoria was on the throne.

Victorian England was a country dominated by class distinctions. The gentry were always in a position to demand specific concessions, as exemplified by this notice:

'Great Western Railway. Notice is hereby given that this level crossing may only be used by members of the Badminton Hunt and other persons when hunting with the Badminton Fox-hounds on horseback or on foot (but not with wheeled vehicles) during the hunting season, and that all such persons using this gate and level crossing, do so at their own risk and responsibility in all respects, and shall not have any right of action, claim, or demand against the company by reason of any damage or injury which may happen to such person or persons or his, her or their horses or hounds, while using this gate or crossing.' February 1900.

On occasion, treasures appeared by pure chance. One donor was looking for a suitably ornate frame for a print that he had at home and found just what he wanted. It contained a Victorian portrait of Emperor Napoleon III, who had been exiled to Britain, where he became quite a popular figure. As the purchaser was not interested in French potentates, he removed the print and discovered another print lurking behind it. It was a track diagram clearly labelled 'Slough Station (East Cabin) Diagram of Signals'. It was coloured and drawn by C. Hills of Saxby & Farmer and dated 29 May 1879. So this puts it in the broad gauge era when the early interlocking signals were being installed by Saxby & Farmer rather than the company's own signals department at Reading. The frame and glass appear to be original and if the diagram had just been kept there it would probably have faded with time, but protected by the emperor, the colours are as fresh and sharp as ever they were. The reference to the East Cabin simply reflects the fact that that is how signal boxes were originally known. In 1985, this valuable item was donated to the Trust.

Other items were acquired by individuals who knew exactly what they were getting. One of these is a £100 ordinary share certificate dated 10 April 1836, originally bought by John Prideaux Esquire of Bristol. It may not sound a lot of money at today's values, but historic currency value converters suggest that it would be equivalent to almost £8,000 today. It is an example of the enthusiasm of Bristolians for the new railway that an individual should be prepared to make such a substantial investment – and for

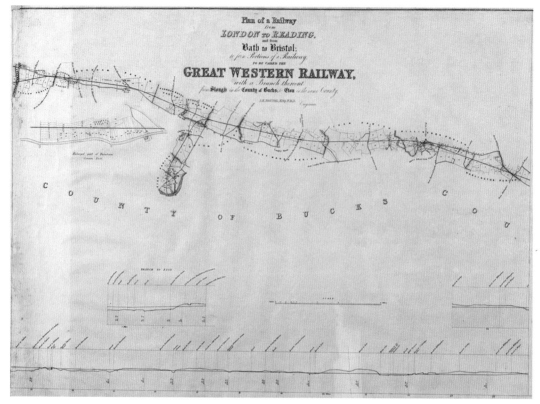

This early map dates right back to the days when the Great Western was first applying to Parliament for a Bill to allow construction to start; it shows the line to Eton that was never built.

all we know, he may even have bought more than one share. This valuable item was bequeathed to the museum by Charles Gordon Stuart and it was by no means his only bequest. He also left his unique collection of railway tickets – all 23,000 of them, together with a bequest of £40,000, which provided the necessary basis for raising the funds to house the extension in which these unique items are now stored.

As the museum became more widely known, more and more offers of material started to come in. It was amazing what people found when clearing out attics and garages, often after a death in the family. One surprising item came from an Australian family who were sorting out their late grandfather's library. He had emigrated in the 1880s. He was not a railway enthusiast – the books were just popular reading. But one of them had a GWR timetable card, obviously brought with him from Britain over a century ago and used as a bookmark. Fortunately, the family recognised its importance and posted it off to Didcot. Often people appear in person at the museum, clutching material that they think should be preserved – often it is sadly of very little interest or simply duplicates material already held. Or they phone up with a rather vague message that they have found some items and could they please bring them in. One such phone call was made by a family who had been doing the usual clear out, but with no real indication of what the items might be, other than railway books and papers, so no one was expecting very much. They arrived with a load of material and one of the items was a GWR rule book which didn't arouse any initial enthusiasm as there were already examples in the collection. But a closer look revealed this to be an absolute gem. This was no ordinary rule book but was dated 1 September 1890 and it had belonged to and was signed by James Inglis. At that time, he was the Resident Engineer overseeing the doubling of the South Devon line to Plymouth. He went on to become General Manager and initiated an important programme of staff training, being credited with coming up with the very catchy title for the train to the south-west – the *Cornish Riviera Express*.

The Society was curious to know how such a historic item came to end up forgotten in an attic. It seems that it had belonged to a former GWR inspector, William Noke. Like many old GWR men, he was horrified when, on nationalisation, the order went out to get rid of all the old material; this was to be a new beginning and there was no room for past glories. So he had simply taken stuff destined for a skip and brought it home. The box was full of his papers and memorabilia and the family donated the whole lot to Didcot.

There are many items in the store relating directly to exhibits on the main display area. One interesting section, for example, deals with the Company's enthusiasm for teaching staff the fundamentals of first aid. This was clearly of great importance in wartime, when railways were under attack from the air. As an added inducement to the staff, medals were handed out annually at the discretion of the GWR's Chief Medical Officer for outstanding work. In 1942, the gold medal was awarded to Harry Westbury, who attended a young woman who had intended to commit suicide and would have bled to death had he not acted promptly and efficiently to stem the bleeding. A doctor who happened to be on the train came along later and wrote to the GWR to say that he had served as a medical officer in the First World War and this was one of the best examples of first aid he had ever seen. The handsome medal was presented by the family for safe keeping in honour of their late relative. Medals and medallions are always of interest, as much for their pictorial value as their provenance. Those which satisfy both criteria are especially interesting. One of these is a silver medal inaugurated by a GWR Director, Lord Winterstoke, as a reward for the best students at the London School of Economics. On one side is a portrait of Brunel and round the rim an image of the Royal Albert Bridge. What makes this especially interesting is that it was awarded to G.W. Chapman, who was to go on to write the very popular GWR *Books for Boys of All Ages* series.

Chapman's books were only a part of a wider movement by the GWR to interest the young in railways in general and their own lines in particular – the young enthusiast would, it was hoped, carry his enthusiasm over into later life. It seems to have started at the Wembley Exhibition of 1924, when it was reported that the GWR stand was surrounded by 'hordes of locusts' in short trousers and school blazers. To encourage these young enthusiasts, the company started producing all kinds of merchandise, starting with a colouring book *All About Railways*. They went on to turn out a wide range of goods from jigsaws to pull along trains. The toys in the collection were another part of Ronald King Bird's legacy.

One last item which comes with a question – why should the Great Western Society want to keep a Director's Free Pass issued to a director of the London & North Eastern Railway? The clue is in the name of the LNER director – the Hon. G. C. Gibbs. Sir Geoffrey Cockayne Gibbs, apart from his railway connection, was also chairman of the merchant bankers Anthony Gibbs & Sons. The Gibbs family had an important part to play in setting up the GWR. George Gibbs was a Merchant Venturer who was a founding member of the Bristol Committee. His cousin, George Henry Gibbs, was the ancestor of G. C. Gibbs, like him chairman of the London merchant bank, and he had joined the London Committee. And both were present at the crucial meeting that approved the prospectus for the new company and gave it the proud name Great Western Railway.

It would be possible to go on for many more pages describing the immense array of fascinating objects, either on display or in storage, but hopefully enough has been written to whet the reader's appetite and encourage those who have not done so before to come along and see the displays for themselves – and perhaps encourage some reader to go and investigate that old cardboard box that has been in the attic for years. Who knows what treasures it might contain?

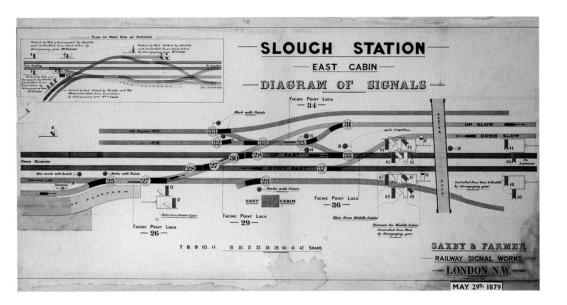

The aim of the museum is to appeal to visitors of all ages, but education has become an important part of the Society's activities – providing educational facilities is a requirement of charitable status. David Bevan was the first educational officer to be appointed and he began an important programme of development. The first item on the agenda was to provide teacher packs. In 2003, these packs were made available on free loan to twenty local schools. This was closely followed in 2004 by the establishment of a set of ten information boards around the site that together form the Archie Learning Trail. This programme was made possible thanks to a £6,000 grant from the Clare Duffield Trust. It was a good start but there was a real need for somewhere that could accommodate a whole class of children. Ideally there would be a purpose-built education centre – and in time there may well be one – but a new centre such as this would have been too expensive to consider at the time. There was, however, a cheaper alternative that became available – a former NNX Parcel Coach. It was decided that this could be fitted out with interactive displays. It was still expensive – the overall budget was costed out at nearly £180,000. Two major grants were applied for; one from the ReDiscover (Millennium) Programme to cover 75 per cent of the costs and another from Biffa awards for roughly 20 per cent. With the successful application, contracts could be awarded for creating the displays. A second redundant coach would act as a classroom, a comparatively simple matter of stripping the interior and putting in tables and chairs. Three local schools that had

This splendid diagram of the layout at Slough was discovered lurking behind an old, rather dull print.

regularly brought classes to the Centre were consulted to ensure that the exhibits were appropriate and fitted in with the schools' requirements. The coach that has been simply laid out with tables and chairs is used for various activities, such as assembling kits to make items such as bridges and locomotives. The second coach uses interactive displays to explain the basic workings of a steam locomotive, starting with the fundamentals of coal, water, fire and steam. From here, it continues to show how steam pressure can cause a piston to move in a cylinder and then how valve gear can be used to turn to and fro motion into rotation. The final display lets the children work out how they must bring all these elements together to make a wheel move.

The centre is, of course, only a part of the learning experience, which includes social history as well as the technology of railways. A popular visit is always to go down into the air raid shelter, where there is a realistic sound track of bombs falling all around outside.

The gold medal awarded to Henry Westbury for his outstanding medical work in saving a young lady's life.

Just outside the shelter is the model railway, which is not merely fun, but can be used in a variety of different ways, as exercises in logic and planning – working out a complex shunting manoeuvre for example.

The educational programme provides a real service for the local community. This has a value in its own right, but it is a vital factor in ensuring support, not least when applying for grants. It is a source of revenue, of course, but it is hoped that it will be far more than that. It is designed to make the centre attractive, interesting and with luck will encourage some at least of the children to want to learn more – perhaps even in time join the Society themselves or take up careers in science or engineering. If Didcot is to continue to be the centre of excellence that it is, then it will need the next generation to come along to continue the work. Providing a good educational experience is to invest in the future.

CHAPTER NINE

Signals and Telegraphy

It is often assumed by outsiders that the only reason to join any type of railway preservation society is to get to drive an engine. There is certainly no shortage of would-be drivers, but anyone turning up at Didcot and expecting to step straight into a footplate role is in for a disappointment. First, the individual will have to show their true enthusiasm for the whole project by working steadily as a volunteer over a period of time. The Society operates much as the railway companies always did in the steam age; start by doing all the dirty jobs – cleaning, ashing out – then with diligence you may become a trainee fireman and after proving your competence you can then apply to learn the skills and acquire the knowledge necessary to become a driver. So perhaps it is as well that not everyone sets out with that as their prime ambition in the first place and within the Bristol group there was a bunch of enthusiasts whose main interest was in signalling and everything that goes with it. They took it upon themselves to introduce historic signalling equipment to Didcot.

At that time, there was no real overall plan or organisation for developing the site; it was more or less up to the individual groups to make their own arrangements, with no absolute need to consult with other groups involved in their own different interests and problems. One can quite see how a passion for signalling could develop. It is indeed a fascinating subject and absolutely crucial to the successful running of any railway. Ultimately, it is on the efficiency of signal control that the safety of the railway depends. Before looking in detail at what has been achieved at Didcot, it is perhaps as well to look at some of the crucial developments in this area – an area in which the GWR played an important role. Indeed, it was an inspector on the Lancashire & Yorkshire Railway who wrote in 1900 that the GWR had 'the most perfectly developed signalling' in Britain. Needless to say, no member of the Bristol group has ever disagreed with that verdict.

The development of signalling was comparatively slow. At the very beginning of the railway age, safety precautions were primitive in the extreme. Rules laid out that there had to be a ten-minute gap

between trains leaving any one point on a line, but that took no account of trains moving at different speeds nor of the possibility of something happening to slow or stop one train in front of another. Maintaining the distance was the job of the railway police, who had a system of hand signals: one arm held out horizontally indicated the way was clear; one hand raised to the vertical was the caution sign; and both hands raised in which the policeman is giving the clear signal called for the train to stop immediately. The system can be seen in the famous illustration of Box tunnel by J.C. Bourne, in which the policeman is giving the clear signal. Instead of a signal box he had a simple shelter, looking very much like a sentry box, an example of which has been erected on site at Didcot.

This was hardly a satisfactory arrangement. The first mechanical signals were introduced on the Liverpool & Manchester Railway in 1834, when night time travel was controlled by a simple system of using lanterns – a red light for stop, green for all clear. The first daytime mechanical signals were introduced at the same time and the GWR was quick to follow with its own system. The first signals consisted of a swivelling red disc on top of a pole: if the disc was facing the driver he had to stop; if it was turned through 90° and thus invisible to him he could carry on. It was later improved by

The Radstock
Road signal box in its original situation.

Sir John Hawkins, who added a cross bar. No signals from this period were available, so when the broad gauge was being laid out at Didcot, it was decided to produce replicas. The disc sits at the top of the tall post, with the crossbar below and at right angles to it. This means that the driver sees only one of them facing his way: if the disc shows, then the line is clear; if the crossbar shows, he must stop. The replica here has two downward pointing tails at the end to tell the driver it is the sign for the down line. The system was still operated by the railway policeman. At Box tunnel, the signal itself was duplicated, fixed to a very long pole, with one set of bar and disc at drivers' level, the other at the top, visible from a distance.

The other form of indicator was devised by Brunel and first installed at Maidenhead in 1839. This capstan signal was worked in conjunction with points. It consists of a short cast iron pedestal with a disc on top: when the points are set for traffic to carry straight on along the main line, the disc automatically turns to face the driver; when set for a diversion, the disc is edge on.

The development of signalling was a very gradual process. The first signal box was installed at Normanton where the York & North Midland from York met the North Midland from Derby. The signalman needed to keep an eye on both tracks to operate

The Radstock box rebuilt at Didcot.

the signals manually to control the junction. Other railways soon followed suit. The once ubiquitous semaphore signals were based on a communication system first developed in France by Claude Chappe in the 1790s. A series of towers with movable arms at the top were used to relay messages all the way from Lille to Paris, a distance of 144 miles. But a far more efficient system of long-distance communication was being developed at much the same time.

The connection between electricity and magnetism had been known for some time; a magnetic needle placed beneath a wire would be moved when a current flowed through the wire – the basis of the galvanometer. A former Indian Army officer, William Fothergill Cooke, realised that this could be the basis for a communication system, but had trouble making a practical device. He took his idea to Professor Charles Wheatsone of King's College, London, a leading authority on electricity. They pooled their resources and came up with the electric telegraph, which they patented in 1837. They used five needles that were deflected to indicate letters on a grid. They showed the device to railway companies, but it was the Great Western that was the first to take up the idea. In 1837, they installed a telegraph between Paddington and West Drayton, later extending it to Slough. Now signalmen could communicate with each other efficiently and as well as being the start of a new age of safety on the railways, it also proved its value in a very different field. A woman was murdered in Slough and a description of the suspect, who was seen getting on a train for London, was telegraphed ahead. When he arrived at Paddington the police were waiting.

The next major step forward came when a new system of train separation was introduced between Yarmouth and Norwich in 1844. Instead of being separated by a time interval, they were kept spatially apart. The line was divided into 'blocks'. Once a train had been admitted to a block by the signalman responsible, he would pass the message on by telegraph to the next signal box. No train was then allowed into that space until the signalman at the far end of the block passed the message back that the train had cleared that section. The next major advance was to link points and signals through levers in the signal box. There would be other improvements over the years but the basis of the block signalling system with semaphore signals, linked points and communication between boxes down the line remained standard for a very long time and it is the system that is still used at the Didcot Centre.

The interior of the Radstock box.

So after that brief, simplified scamper through signalling history, it is time to return to what did happen at Didcot.

The enthusiasts in the Bristol group started with the very modest ambition of acquiring a signal, which was duly achieved. The closure of the Bristol to Radstock line was announced in 1968. The line had largely been used for freight trains serving the local collieries but these were in terminal decline. The local authority was also very keen to see the removal of the two level crossings that caused congestion on the routes into town – a problem that was partially solved when a runaway set of coal wagons demolished one gate a little later. So a signal was available from the area and was duly removed in May 1972. With one success under their belts, the Bristolians now decided that a signal needed a signal box and the GWS Council approved the idea. They scoured the local area, looked at several alternatives, but eventually decided that the best choice would be Radstock North. After that, the lengthy business of negotiation got under way.

The first stage was to approach British Rail to find out if they were prepared to sell the box when it became available and they agreed to let the Society have first refusal. Nothing very much happened for a year, but when the group's secretary, John Lakey, wrote to the County Council asking if there were any road plans for the immediate area, things started to move forward. In September

1975, there was a meeting with the Council and BR, during which the box was offered to the Society and the Council agreed to buy the land for road improvement. In September, a formal agreement was reached that the box would be sold for £54 (just over £300 at today's prices) and the money duly went off. The only snag was the time scale; there were only eight weeks in which to organise the removal of a wooden building 18ft by 12ft and 10ft high together with the essential machinery– and, of course, to start making preparations for its restoration and re-erection.

Working parties met at weekends, starting on Sunday, 12 October 1975, sometimes working Saturdays as well as Sundays. As time pressures grew, a party of stalwarts spent a night working under the harsh glare of a single Tilley lamp, drilling holes for bolts and screws to strengthen the corners of the wooden, upper part of the box in preparation for the move. There was a great deal of work to be done. The locking frame had to be bolted to supporting wooden beams. All the leading off beds had to be disconnected and the rodding, cranks and steps removed. The level crossing gate and a telegraph pole were also removed. The inside was reinforced with scaffolding, the guttering and bottom row of slates removed from the roof and the rest of the slates tested to make sure they were firmly attached. Finally, the vent on the roof had to be removed to reduce the overall height to less than 14 feet, the maximum height of a load that could be taken on the road without a special movement order.

Everything was ready for the big removal day, Sunday, 23 November. At 7am, the 22-ton crane trundled onto the site, and the first of two low loaders was positioned next to the box. The steel lifting beams were positioned under the wooden box to support the main timbers at each side and the crane jib extended. The shackles were connected to the lifting beams and the slack taken up, ready for the lift. Inside the box, John Lakey, Derek Fear and Kevin Evans knocked out the four spacing blocks, fitted between the floorboard beams and the locking frame, and scurried out before the whole structure became airborne. It was then lifted free of the brick base and raised a further five feet to clear the lever frame. Then it was swung onto the low loader. There was space for several other items – steps, gate wheel assembly, step rails and wicket gates and once they were all secure the low loader was removed and parked up. By 10.30 it was on its way with a police escort.

The brick wall was now unsafe and had to be demolished, but the specially shaped blue engineering bricks round the windows were preserved. It has always been Society policy to try and preserve the look of original buildings as far as possible, and modern bricks are very different from those in use years ago. Window frames from the lower brick section and locking room door were also saved. Once that was complete, the second low loader was brought into position and the two-ton lever frame with its wooden supporting frame were swung out and settled in place. The level crossing gates, lifting beds, rodding and several other items were added and that load too set off. Unlike the first load, which had a speed restriction of 15-20mph and a police escort, the second load had no speed restrictions and was the first to arrive on site at Didcot. By the time the main structure arrived, the first trailer was already half unloaded. A working party had been left behind at Radstock to clear up the site, while the rest had driven back in three cars to be ready for the arrival of the first load. The removal had been a complete success. Now there remained the task of reassembling it.

Because groups were still acting independently rather than as part of an organised plan for the site as a whole, it was rather a case of identifying a likely location and then laying claim to it. Having selected a site and got approval, the first stage was to lay the concrete base. After that, the brickwork could begin for the base – a job this time for the professionals. The shaped bricks that had been rescued from Radstock were brought back into use, and a donation of more engineering bricks meant that a very satisfactory approximation to the original base was constructed, using window frames and doors saved from the demolition process. With the base complete, the wooden superstructure could be brought out of storage and set in place. This time, however, there was no contractor on site with a massive crane to do the job. So the whole job was down to volunteers and workers supplied by the Manpower Services Scheme that was then in operation. The work involved using a variety of tools – boiler tubes, for example, had to make do as rollers for moving the box around. Lifting was by crowbars, screw jacks and a great deal of packing timber. It took two days of really hard, physical effort before the wooden top was firmly settled in place. There was still a lot of work to be done, including supplying new steps as the box had originally been approached from the raised platform, not from ground level, and the old steps were now too short.

The lever frame that was in the box has been dated as having been installed in 1896. This is a 24-lever double-twist locking frame, a type that was manufactured by the GWR themselves

between 1890 and 1906. The term double-twist refers to the rotating system that connects the levers to the locking mechanism. By early December 1980, everything was complete but a signal box with no array of signals nor anything else to operate has no function. It was not until May 1985 that it was truly operational, controlling the level crossing, one set of points and a solitary signal. Today, as the rail system has grown ever more complex, the signal box is fully operational – and an essential for special days when more than one locomotive is in steam.

As work on Radstock neared completion, the search was on for the next big project. An essential of the block signalling system is that a train is passed on from one signal box to the next down the line and nothing else can enter that section until it has been cleared by the second box. Clearly this cannot be demonstrated satisfactorily if you only have the one box, so it was agreed to look for another.

The first question to be decided was – what type of box was needed? Whatever was chosen would have to be comparatively small as space at Didcot was limited, accessible for easy removal and preferably made in Reading. At this point the Taunton group

The rather dilapidated Frome Junction box on its original site.

stepped into the discussion with a request that the box should be from the broad gauge era to complete their plans for installing a mixed gauge system. British Rail announced that they were engaging in a major transformation of signalling in their Western Region, so various boxes would become redundant. The first choice was the box at Bruton but for a variety of technical reasons it was eventually dismissed as unsuitable, so the decision was to go for the second choice, Frome North. Unlike Radstock, this was largely brick built, with the base extended upwards to form the back wall of the box up to roof level. As the wooden structure only occupied three sides, it had to be reinforced with stout timbers all round in order to move it without the whole structure collapsing.

The box was closed on 6 October 1984, which left the volunteers with three weeks to demolish the brickwork, remove the roof, creosoting it for protection, and secure the frame ready for the lift on Sunday the 28th. It was not straightforward, as the nearby main road had to be closed for three hours while the crane was operating and overhead electricity cables had to be isolated. In the event, everything went smoothly; the crane arrived at nine in the morning and the lorry departed on schedule with the box and other material

The Frome box at Didcot.

saved from the site. As always at Didcot, nothing can be brought on site by road, so arrangements had to be made to continue the final part of the journey by rail. So on Monday morning, everyone was waiting at the local provender yard with the rail wagon, signal box crew and a loading inspector. Unfortunately, one essential item was missing – the crane to complete the move from lorry to wagon was absent. It arrived three hours later, by which time the shunters had left for lunch. It was 2.30 before the box set off on the last leg of its journey at a stately 5mph.

Once in position, the job of restoration could get under way. New window frames were installed, a set of steps to the original design added and new slates put on the roof. Once that was completed, the box could be fitted out and made the centrepiece of the broad gauge section. Together with the landscaping of the surrounding area, the installation of signal box and signalling added the finishing touch to this important recreation of a part of railway history that came to an end over a century ago.

The work of the signals group received official recognition in 1990 when the Radstock box received the annual ARPS/Ian Allan award for the best signal box restoration. The judges wrote:

'This entry of a small country signal box and level crossing is particularly impressive. The standard of work was high and has been applied consistently throughout. There was nothing to detract from the general ambience of the scene. The decision to construct a gated level crossing to accompany the signal box is to be commended as such things will, before long, be a thing of the past.'

The comments were well deserved – but the prophecy not quite accurate. At least one gated and manned level crossing has survived at Chalford, between Stroud and Kemble.

Over the years, signalling has been added to the site and one of the aims was to provide as many different types of signal as possible to give an indication of the variety that was once present throughout the whole system and how designs changed over time. As far as possible, they are constructed of original material. Each of them has its own story and points of interest, as the next few examples should make clear. The name and number refer to the signal box controlling them and the number on the lever in that box used for operating them.

The signal Frome 1/2 is a design from the 1870s, when signals were provided by McKenzie and Holland. The two men had purchased a patent for a locking frame and arranged to go into business manufacturing signals at the Vulcan Engineering Works, set up in Worcester by Thomas Clunes. The first signals were produced from the works in 1862. This is a slotted post signal; when the road was clear the signal arm was tucked away out of sight inside the post. In other words, provided the driver saw no signal, then he could assume the way ahead was clear. A raised signal was a sign to stop. This system turned out to be far from perfect. On the cold night of 21 January 1876 on the Great Northern Railway when visibility was reduced by snowstorms, a slow goods train with 37 coal wagons was trundling south from Peterborough. The signalman was supposed to stop it and move it into a siding to allow a fast express to overtake on the main line and he pulled off the appropriate lever. What he could not have known was that the signal was frozen into its slot, so the goods train driver simply assumed the road ahead was clear. The inevitable result was that the express ploughed into the back of the goods. That was bad enough, but the next express coming in the opposite direction from London smashed into the wreckage. The result was a tragedy in which fourteen people were killed and twenty-four seriously injured. After that, the system was changed so that there were definite signals from the signal arms. The other interesting point about this signal is that it originally sat at a junction, so there are two arms – the upper arm applying to the left hand route, the lower to the right. The whole is topped by a decorative McKenzie and Holland finial.

Radstock 20 Frome 4 is a designation that indicates that this is a signal that is controlled by both boxes – in order to operate it, levers have to be pulled in each of them. The other feature is the semi-circular white board behind the arm. This is a sighting board, which is used when the signal has a dark background, such as a dense mass of foliage, making it difficult to see. Radstock 2 is an example of how outside influences can affect design. In 1917, when Europe was at war, there was a severe shortage of timber so a cheap alternative had to be found. The answer was to use a concrete post, in this case made at the Taunton Concrete Works. It has a simple wooden arm, but with a white ring at the end to show that it was in use on a goods line or loop. By the late 1920s, concrete had given way to metal posts as can be seen on one of the more elaborate signals – Radstock 3/5.

The semaphore arms work well in daylight but when night falls, the other part of the signal comes into use – the spectacle plate. This has coloured glasses to indicate clear ahead or stop, which are covered or uncovered appropriately. A lantern behind the spectacle plate means that the driver sees a bright green or red light as he approaches. On most open days there is no need for this arrangement, but at Christmas when Thomas the Tank Engine might put in an appearance or Santa Specials run into the night, the staff have to fill the oil lamps and light them at dusk. This system of signals lit by oil lamps was still in use as late as the 1950s when I had a holiday job as a porter and one of my first jobs on the early shift was to walk down the line and refill the lamps. Lamps themselves were kept in a lamp hut, a very

A double signal used to control movement at a junction.

Replica signals from the broad gauge era: the simplest form was the disc. If the disc faced the driver it was a stop sign; if turned though 90° so that it was edge-on, he could proceed.

basic structure indeed – so basic indeed that when it became redundant the hut from Tetbury station was removed and used as a garden shed. Fortunately, someone recognised its historic importance, and it was donated to the Society. A standard 9ft by 6ft lamp hut was spotted at Frome station goods yard, and the iron frame brought back to Didcot, where it was given a new corrugated iron cladding. These structures may be plain and unobtrusive and most visitors probably pass them by without showing much interest, but they had an important part to play

in the running of the railways. Without the lamps, then no night running would be possible.

Not all the signals are stuck up on posts; a variety of others can be seen at ground level, performing different functions. Probably the simplest is the Ground Stop Board; it simply says 'Stop' on one side – a message that needs no further explanation. Radstock 8 is rather more complex. Dating from around 1918, this has an enamel disc with a red diagonal stripe. It has a rod connecting it to the blade of a point. When the point is operated, the signal will only give a clear way if the blade has fitted home correctly. The various ground-based signals may not be as striking as the semaphore signals, but they do add to the rich variety of equipment that the interested visitor can enjoy – and even the casual visitor might well be intrigued and want to know more.

Special arrangements have to be made for sections of single line working; you obviously cannot have two trains travelling in opposite directions on the same length of track. So a system had to be devised that would ensure this could not happen by locking the points at either end of the section, so that if a train had entered from one end, the locked points at the far end could not be operated. At Didcot, this is represented by the Webb-Thompson Electric Train Staff system. The staff is a heavy metal tube, roughly 2ft in length. When, and only when, it is inserted into the mechanism, can the points be worked. When a train is admitted onto a single line section, the staff is handed to one of the footplate crew and it is carried on to the ends of the section, where it is handed over so that the signalman at the far end can then operate his points when the train has safely cleared the section. Instruments have been set up in both the Frome and Radstock signal boxes.

An extra safety measure was introduced by the GWR in 1913. This was the Automatic Train Control (ATC). It had two elements, one on the train itself, the other on the track. An air inlet valve attached to the vacuum brakes on the locomotive is kept closed by electric magnets in normal service and the electric circuit contains a switch located in a metal shoe below the engine. This is held roughly two inches above the rails. The other element is a ramp between the rails. This too is supplied with an electric current. When the shoe passes over the ramp while the current is on, the circuit remains intact. If, however, the current to the ramp has been switched off, the circuit will be broken, the air inlet will open, destroying the vacuum, bringing the brakes into operation and sounding a warning bell in the cab. An example of an ATC ramp can be seen on the main running line at Didcot.

Although visitors can see signals and signal boxes, it is difficult to arrange for anyone to see the actual workings of either box, simply because there is so little space inside. It was decided that to give everyone a more complete picture of how the system developed and how it worked a special exhibition area would be needed. This was to be the Train Control Centre and it would require a new building to be added to the site. As always at Didcot, a great deal of care was taken to create a structure that was in keeping with the site and reflected GWR design features. That involved collecting together discarded items from old railway buildings, such as typical, segmented arch, iron-framed windows that in time would be neatly topped by a curving pattern of blue engineering bricks. Doors were salvaged from different sources but all come from railway buildings. But before any of these could be put in place, the building needed a solid foundation and at Didcot that always creates a special problem. The ground on site is a mixture of locomotive ash and loose spoil from civil engineering works. So the decision was taken to create a massive foundation of concrete aggregate base, reinforced concrete and binding concrete. This work was carried out by a group of 25 volunteers who started on the process in the autumn of 2014 and poured the final concrete in the following spring. By the time the foundations were finished, they contained just over 174 tonnes of steel and concrete – which, as a note in the *Echo* pointed out, was heavier than a King locomotive. Once again, in the determination to make the building as authentic as possible, it was decided that the brick walls should appear to be laid with English bond, consisting of alternate layers of headers (the short side) and stretchers (the long side). Unfortunately, this method of bricklaying cannot be used if you need to install modern cavity wall insulation, but the same appearance can be achieved, by using half bricks to simulate the headers. You can't go out and buy half bricks, so once again volunteers were called in to carry out the laborious work of cutting bricks using a basic hand-operated cutter. The actual work of building the walls and roof was left to professional contractors.

With the building secure and watertight, the job of installing exhibitions could begin. The aim is to provide a potted history of signalling practices from the earliest times up to the modern age. So the first items that the visitor will see date back to the start of the broad gauge era, when policemen operated hand levers to

work signals and points. We then move on to the next stage of development of block working, semaphore signals and locking for points and signals, with a display featuring block equipment and two levers on a frame. A visitor can pull these – one works a signal just outside the window and the other one inside the building. The next exhibit shows the replacement of the old signals by coloured lamps. Up to this stage, everything has been manual and communication between signalmen had been by telegraph and coded bells. At the next stage, we leap forward to the 1930s and electro-mechanical systems. The actual overall pattern remains the same – it still depends on controlling a block through locked signals and points, but now electric systems have been introduced, represented by the track diagram from Bristol East signal box. The signalman no longer needs to communicate with his colleagues down the line, because the diagram shows exactly what is happening on each part of the system covered by the diagram. Here all the lines are laid out just as they are on the ground and a system of lights indicates what is happening on each section and which trains are where. But the operative still has to pull handles to operate the system. When completed, the aim is to show a typical day at Bristol Temple Meads, with the movement of trains represented by the 250 light

In the late twentieth century, electric relays replaced the old manual system. This panel controlled movements at Swindon station. Modern electronics have made it obsolete and it is now in the new signalling exhibition at Didcot.

bulbs, tracing the different pathways in and out of the station. This would later be superseded by more efficient all electric signalling, known as MAS – multiple aspect signalling.

The Bristol East diagram could well have been the last exhibit in the story, but a quite different group with an interest in signalling, but quite independent of the GWS, had been formed in 2013 – the Swindon Panel Society. The twenty-first century is the age of electronics and it was inevitable that the electric system too would have its day. As a result, the panel at Swindon was due for replacement and the Society decided it needed to be saved. Their first thought was to obtain a container and put it in that, but when they heard about the new Train Control Centre at Didcot, they realised at once that this would be a far better home and the GWS were equally happy to make them welcome. The Swindon Panel volunteers showed their enthusiasm for joining in from the start – and they worked alongside the GWS gang in preparing the foundations of the building. Although agreement had been reached as early as 2013 to buy the panel for the princely sum of £1 – with, of course, the proviso it was up to the Society to pay for its removal – it had to remain in use until the replacement electronics were up and running.

It was April 2017 before the panel became available. It then had to be placed on supports before it could finally be moved, first by truck to Didcot and then the final part of the journey by rail. It is perhaps ironic that this piece of equipment that represented the modernisation of the railway system ended its journey to its new home being moved by a steam crane. Now installed at Didcot, it is a fascinating device. The whole structure is some thirty foot long and the main panel shows the route either side of Swindon, stretching almost to Didcot in one direction, and as far as Chippenham in the other and a section of the line to Cheltenham, together with all the tracks and points. This is created as a jigsaw made up of hundreds of 40mm square tiles, known as 'dominos'. This is a system patented by a Swiss company. Some of the squares are blanks, others that coincide with signals and points have switches. So if, for example, a train is approaching from Didcot, it can be switched either to continue on towards Bristol or moved further north to the Cheltenham line. If there is a clear road, the appropriate track lights up. It all looks simple enough on the outside but go round the back of the panel and you can see the complexity of the whole thing. It is a vast networked mass of wires, each of which has to be soldered to the right terminal so that relays can activate the appropriate points and signals.

Swindon Panel Society

At its new home at the Centre, the panel will no longer be wired up to work lights and signals along the track, but instead will be attached to a computer. Software will be used to simulate various situations. Visitors can have a go at controlling the system – and will be thrown the occasional problem to solve – perhaps a driver reporting a cow on the line. The array is completed by the supervisor's desk, which also contains the train announcement system. It looks like proving a hugely popular item with visitors, though at the time of writing it was just nearing completion in preparation for the official opening date in June 2018. That is not quite the end of the story, for just across from the Radstock level crossing is the modern traffic control centre at Didcot. So in just a short walk, visitors can move from the age of the hand-signalling policeman to the electronic age. This is the one part of the site where a decision has been taken to go beyond the golden age of the Great Western Railway, through the years of nationalisation and on into the railway world of today.

The back of the Swindon panel, showing the complexity of the wiring.

CHAPTER TEN

Trips and Tours

No matter how fine a collection of locomotives and rolling stock you have and no matter how interesting they may be in their own rights, as any visitor to Didcot today can testify, there is nothing quite like seeing them on the move. Even to those who have absolutely no knowledge of steam engines, the sight of a majestic locomotive slowly gathering speed is hypnotic. The intricate movement of connecting rods and pistons, the hiss of escaping steam are always memorable. Equally, to ride behind a steam locomotive is a very different experience from travelling in a modern train. The steam locomotive has a beating heart and just by listening to the sound of the exhaust the passenger knows just how the locomotive is performing. Just like most of us, a locomotive breathes easily moving along the flat, but starts to pant going uphill. And just like us, things sometimes go wrong; wheel slip at the start of a run brings sad shakes of the head from the knowledgeable passengers – not to mention annoyance and a flash of embarrassment to the driver. So from the start, one of the main aims of the Society was to get locomotives into a condition when they could be steamed and to bring carriages into a fit state to be used for passengers. As will be clear from earlier chapters, this does not happen without a great deal of hard work. And the hard work does not end there; a locomotive is not like your car where you simply sit down and turn a key and then you're ready to go. But the effort required to make an engine move is hugely rewarding for all concerned, and even in the earliest days one of the main efforts went into sharing the experience of travelling by steam with the public at large.

When the Society first moved into Didcot and still had stock at Taplow, it was anticipated that the main function of the former would be to provide cover for the stock and some workshop facilities. A Newsletter of the time noted that there was a small branch line on which trains could be operated occasionally 'primarily for the enjoyment of Society members'. It would not be long before more ambitious plans would be hatched. But the first public steamings were not held at Didcot. There was an Operating

Day at Taplow on Easter Monday 1968. The Newsletter for April made a plea for members to support the event – it was in fact only advertised to members. There was no need to worry. On the day, 1,400 enthusiasts turned up. A shuttle service was run between Cholsey and Wallingford – though not into Wallingford Station – with 1466 and the auto coach, even though neither had been fully restored. Nevertheless, a total of twenty round trips were made and passengers could enjoy the ride and a photo stop for the princely sum of 2/6 and 1/6 for children. Another open day in September was advertised in local papers, not just to members, and attracted far larger crowds. Unfortunately, there were delays in getting started. It had been intended to erect a temporary platform of sleepers to make getting on and off the train easier – but when the crew arrived to do the work they discovered all the material was at Cholsey. There were long queues for the train rides and far too many potential customers for the little train to manage – half went away disappointed. The obvious lesson was that an extra coach

6106 taking on water at Taplow before going into service.

was urgently needed. A bonus laid on for the visitors was a coach shuttle to Didcot to see the rest of the Society's stock.

The operating days were deemed a great success but immediately afterwards British Rail imposed a ban on all privately owned steam trains running over their tracks. As a result, on the next open day the best that could be offered was a round trip to the Wallingford Carnival in a hired DMU. Taplow's days of steam glory were ended. But the following year saw 1466 steaming again, this time at its new home at Didcot. The first Didcot open day was held on 10 May 1969 but was deliberately kept small scale and again only advertised to members. Locomotives and rolling stock were on display outside the shed. It was a very mixed collection with *Bonnie Prince Charlie*, *Shannon* and the diesel rail car on static display, 6106 in steam and the ever reliable 1466 giving short rides on a siding. Star of the carriage collection was Ocean coach 9118, proudly displaying the new gold lettering on the side with the name *Princess Elizabeth*. The day was declared a success on all counts – the visitors enjoyed the experience and the Society made a profit. It was just the start of what were to prove many more and increasingly ambitious events.

1972 proved to be a momentous year for Didcot. Thanks to the success of previous open days, it was decided to extend the May event to have the first open weekend that would also invite in the general public. It promised to be a highly successful affair. A new running road, number 8, had recently been completed – a great improvement on the old number 5 – and there was to be a visiting locomotive on display, the former LNER A2 Pacific *Blue Peter*. What no one had anticipated was that it would coincide with industrial action. No trains ran from Paddington after 2 o'clock on the Saturday afternoon. Typically, the Society rallied to the emergency. Tannoy messages went out asking for lifts for stranded visitors and a member brought along a vintage bus to give rides to Oxford. In spite of the problems, some 6,000 turned up over the weekend, and enjoyed rides on the new line behind *Pendennis Castle* and *Blue Peter* somehow did make it into Didcot in spite of all the troubles. A pattern was established for regular weekend opening with locomotives in steam. Later this would be extended, and in 1976 there was the steam week that among the other visitors included some 5,000 school children, many of whom had never seen a steam engine before. It was a success, though one visitor wrote in to complain there were too many people there – he couldn't get them to move out of his way so he could take photographs.

The vintage train at Weymouth.

More worryingly was the strain it put on volunteer resources – at one time there was only one person to look after all the catering. The lesson was obvious – more would be needed if essential standards were to be maintained.

The ban on steam on British Rail tracks had been lifted and on 10 June, 7029 *Clun Castle* steamed into Didcot station. The locomotive was moved to the centre, offering the rare sight of the three Castles lined up together – *Clun Castle*, *Pendennis Castle* and *Earl Bathurst*. The next day, *Clun Castle* was coupled up to a 1947 GWR Special Saloon and returned to the main line for an excursion to Tyseley. Only one incident slightly marred the trip, when two passengers turned out not to have tickets and refused to pay – they were turned off the train at Oxford. It was now time for a special Didcot excursion. On 1 October, No 6998 *Burton Agnes Hall* pulled into Didcot station hauling two Collett coaches; 1289 the 'Excursion' coach with its very fine Art Deco interior and 5952, a rather more traditional third class carriage. The train was completed by the addition of eight British Rail coaches brought up from Paddington by a Hymek diesel-hydraulic engine. The whole excursion to Tyseley and back was an immense success, with the train filled to capacity. There were a few very minor hiccups, such as being held up by signals and the need to replace a split pin in a cross head at Tyseley, but otherwise everything went smoothly. The BR driver and firemen were thanked for the efficient running of the train. It was also a very useful exercise in public relations – for example, the train was held long enough at Oxford on the outward journey to allow several interested spectators to get a proper chance to see steam back on the line and there was a photo stop at Heyford. Most importantly of all, it demonstrated that the Society was capable of organising a steam excursion over British Rail tracks

A rare sight – chocolate and cream coaches at Paddington.

and set a good precedent for future events. Fortunately, this was a view shared by British Rail who promised to make more route miles available for steam.

All this was good news, but it had implications for the future. Although Society membership had been growing healthily, there was still a shortage of volunteers to carry out essential work. Half the locomotives in stock were awaiting restoration to full working order. Preparing locomotives and rolling stock for rail tours was far more demanding than merely preparing them for running on site; very high standards were required before anything could be moved over British Rail tracks. This was demonstrated when it came time to prepare for a momentous event in September 1974 – the first tour in which everything, locomotives and rolling stock, would be supplied by Didcot.

Before the run was authorised, British Rail had to be satisfied that the locomotives were in perfect condition. Two inspectors turned up at Didcot – one to check the mechanical state of the engines and the other the boilers. 6998 *Burton Agnes Hall* gave no problems, but 7898 *Cookham Manor* failed an essential check. The safety valve fluttered between 205 and 225psi, which was unacceptable for a locomotive with a normal working pressure of 225psi, so the locomotive was sent off to Swindon works where the whole unit was reconditioned. Whilst there, the locomotive was run onto the weight house to check the readings on all the springs, which were then adjusted. Work completed, 7898 returned to Didcot ready for duty. With the locomotives confirmed as ready for work, it was decided it would be advisable to check the coaches. Earlier in the year, coaches 1289 and 1111 had been presented to British Rail inspectors for approval for fast running on the main line. Unfortunately, tests on 1111 revealed a flaw in one wheel set that then had to be replaced. The test run would confirm that everything was now in order. The carriages were run to Oxford and back behind a diesel and no problems occurred. They were passed by the British Rail Carriage and Wagon Inspector. The line up was now complete, with the two approved locomotives and a train made up of carriages 9118, 1289, 7313, 536, 5952, 1111 and 7372. So now everything was ready and in order.

On the evening of the 18th, both engines were lit up as a final check. The coaches were marshalled into the correct order and steam heated by 6998. Early the next morning, everything was cleaned, polished and lubricated ready for the BR drivers and firemen who arrived at 9 am together with two BR inspectors. The train then moved out into Didcot. The run went smoothly as far as Tyseley, where there was time for passengers to look round before returning to Didcot. The only thing that went wrong was at Oxford, when the train was halted on the middle road so that meant no one could get off, and arrangements had to be made to return some people to Oxford after arriving at Didcot. This was a minor inconvenience for what was otherwise a highly successful venture – and one that took place just ten years to the day from the very first open day back at Totnes. The Society had come a very long way in its first decade.

Steam runs were soon covering new ground. In 1975, 6998 and 7808 were back at work after a certain amount of maintenance work and the fixing of a few niggling problems pointed out by BR inspectors. This was a new route, out through Worcester to Hereford and back and it also saw the debut of the Super Saloon 'Queen Mary'

A stop for an excursion train at Tyseley with the crowd coming for a closer look at *Burton Agnes Hall* on the left and *Clun Castle* on the right.

together with its kitchen. A few lucky passengers could relive the pleasures of luxury travel 1930s style with refreshments served at their tables. This was the start of a series of successful runs with vintage trains and were much appreciated by everyone who travelled on them. Understandably, coaches were only allowed to run when in good condition and that involved periodic overhauls and that did not seem to be a problem. But then British Rail dropped something of a bombshell. It announced that all such overhauls had to be carried out by approved agents – and the only approved agents were British Rail's own engineering workshops. It was estimated that this would cost between £5,000 and £6,000 per vehicle – and that was money the Society could simply not afford. In 1979, they had to announce that no more vintage trains made up from the Society's rolling stock would be running on main line routes.

The vintage train was not the only activity that had come to an end. The Taunton group had lost their stock depot and were now working on the broad gauge project at Didcot, but they still had a local Christmas celebration and their own unique rail excursion. They celebrated Christmas 1987 with a party at Crowcombe station, courtesy of the West Somerset Railway, but some members felt that it would be incomplete without a rail excursion – not by steam but by muscle power with their own pump trolley. They set off from Bishop's Lydeard in the rain with a crew of eight enthusiastic pumpers and headed south to Norton Fitzwarren. Then they turned back for Crowcombe and all went well until near Crowcombe station, when everyone was pumping hard, the levers were going up and down but the wheels were not turning. A connecting nut had come loose. They made it into Crowcombe, but not every establishment is equipped with a spanner capable of turning a 4 inch wide nut. But Taunton members are nothing if not ingenious. Someone spotted the 45mph speed limit sign and noticed that the gap between the horizontal of the figure 4 and the crossbar was precisely the necessary 4 inches. The nut was duly tightened, but it is no easy matter using an improvised spanner when it's still attached to an 8 foot long pole. This little adventure may not go down as the most magnificent of the Society's rail tours, but it is certainly one of the oddest.

There has already been a mention of the need to ensure everything is in full working order for both rail excursions and open days, but that is only a part of the story. Everything has to look at its very best when visitors are paying to see locomotives and rolling stock.

Locomotives may start a run spotless but they do not finish up that way, so when they are wanted again someone has to do the hard work. In the Newsletter for April 1988, there was an entertaining piece by Ann Davies on her part in the preparations – one of a series she wrote on the subject.

Following steam tests, the shed was full of decidedly dirty engines, and she started off on 5051, whose green paint was lost to sight below a covering of soot and coal dust. She began the job on 14 February – not perhaps everyone's dream way of spending Valentine's Day. Apparently, one advantage of working on a Castle is the fact that the steam pipes and nameplate are useful aids in clambering up to the top of the engine. Once up there, however, a new hazard appears – if you stand up you are liable to hit your head on a coal chute, releasing yet more clouds of soot. Scraping away at the sooty deposits is a weary business – it took a week to get down to the paintwork – and some parts of the locomotive are more troublesome than others: the greasy parts in front of the cylinders have to be scrubbed with paraffin and the streaks on the boiler caused by acid rain have to be removed. One of the attractive features of a Castle is the large amount of gleaming brass work – attractive, that is, unless you are the one with the Brasso. And somehow, it seems that at the end of the day when you climb down from the engine, you spot the bit you've missed. And at the end of it when the engine is gleaming you can't expect much in the way of praise. A typical comment – 'That's very nice. What about the rest?' So she moved on to other locomotives. At that time the engine shed leaked, so in heavy rain, the mixture of oil, paraffin and rain produces a white slurry and work has to stop. Happily, that was rectified but not until 2010 when a new roof was in place. Nevertheless by 26 March all was done except that 5051 had started to look a bit grubby again. She ended her piece with this plea:

'I am really quite happy working on my own but if there are any reasonably sensible adults out there who wouldn't mind working with someone who is not rose tinted and is quite short tempered, rather carefree and goes on lots of rail tours, come down any weekend in dirty clothes, bearing rags, Brasso, scrubbing brushes, etc., and ask for Ann Davies.'

Cleaning engines was only one of many tasks that needed to be carried out when locomotives were steamed. Work starts early on a steam day. The fire has to be lit long before the engine is needed and gradually built up and carefully tended to raise pressure in a controlled manner. I have a copy of a manual for locomotive drivers which is undated, but as it gives the Stirling Single as an example of the latest in express locomotive designs, and as that was introduced in 1870, one can hazard a guess that it came out somewhere towards the end of the nineteenth century. The author's thoughts on preparation show how little has changed in this respect:

'If a fireman allows himself an abundance of time to get his engine ready, works with heart and soul, works as though the engine would stop, fail, and get short of steam if it was not for his exertions, depend upon it, such a one is destined to make his mark on the foot-plate.'

And there are, of course, many other tasks to perform; lubrication to be seen to and checks to be carried out. Similarly, at the end of the run, it is not simply a case of stopping, getting out and going home. The fire has to be dropped, the grate cleaned and the ashes disposed of. There is a lot of hard, dirty work that the passengers

A fine double heading with *Cookham Manor* in the lead followed by *Burton Agnes Hall.*

never see, but which is absolutely essential. Fortunately at Didcot, there are young volunteers ready to take on these tasks.

The successful running of an open day or a tour requires far more people than just those on the footplate, and there are other specialist jobs for which volunteers have to be trained, such as acting as guards. It is a mark of the enthusiasm shown for such work that one volunteer, Laura Donaldson, spent her 21st birthday on a guards' training day. She got a special birthday present after the public had all gone home; she was allowed to drive 5322 on the main demonstration line.

Didcot's locomotives were never confined to the Society's own runs, many making regular appearances in different parts of the country. In 2006, for example, No 5051 was booked by Aviva trains to run a trip from Cardiff to Fishguard Harbour to celebrate the centenary of the opening of the Great Western route to the harbour. It was to be a double-headed train with *Rood Ashton Hall* completing the partnership. Locomotives also 'go on holiday' to other preserved lines.

Although the emphasis at Didcot has always been on the steam era, it was decided in 1987 that it would be a good idea to have an open day devoted to diesels. One reason was the availability of a Foster Yeoman Class 59 – and this would be the only public appearance. These were a novelty in that for the first time diesels were being introduced into the country that had been made not in the UK but in America. They were based on a very successful design introduced by the Electro-Motive Division of General Motors, adapted to the British loading gauge and with a cab from the BR Class 56. The latter made it easier for the British drivers to adapt to the new engines. As the first of the class had only arrived in Britain in 1986, it was felt that there would be a great deal of interest among diesel enthusiasts. Various other diesels were promised at various times, but many fell by the wayside. Nevertheless, there were enough visitors guaranteed to put in an appearance to make everyone hopeful that the day would be a success.

When the event opened on the foggy morning of 24 October, there was a good line up. The Diesel and Electric group had been busy getting Hymek D7018 and D1035 *Western Yeoman* ready for the occasion. Deltic D9000 *Royal Scots Grey*, English Electric Type 4 D335 and the 59 Class 001 were on hand. Rides were given behind the English Electric D335 from Tyseley and the Deltic. The Didcot

diesel railcar ran all day. The whole day was declared to be a great success – and it was even rumoured that it was much enjoyed by steam enthusiasts as well.

An excursion to Abingdon; a scene that cannot be repeated as the line has closed and the station demolished.

A major change came to the rail system in the 1990s with the privatisation of British Rail, a process that was completed in 1997. It brought with it stricter regulations from the start but steam excursions were still able to go ahead. In 2001, however, more new and stringent regulations came into force. All locomotives coming back into service after an overhaul now had to comply with every single regulation covering current standards or get an exemption certificate from an authorised body, which in the case of Didcot locomotives meant applying to English, Welsh & Scottish Railways (EWS). A first estimate suggested there were some seventy standards that had to be met, about half of which would require an immense amount of work – a process expected to take months rather than weeks. An immediate casualty was that the 2001 Spring Tour with 5051 had to be deferred while everything was sorted out. Running rail tours was getting more complex and inevitably more expensive.

While rail tours became ever more difficult, the number of steam days at Didcot was steadily increasing. The Society has always been on the lookout for ways of attracting more visitors to steam days. One of the great successes over the years has been Thomas days, featuring the much-loved engine created by the Rev. W. Awdry. Among the most successful open days, those featuring Thomas have always been among the most popular. The original Thomas was a locomotive that would otherwise be considered rather commonplace. Built by Hudswell Clarke of Leeds in 1947 for the British Sugar Corporation of Peterborough, No 1800 is a standard 0-6-0 side tank. Like the fictional original, 1800 had always had a bright blue livery, but in 1972, the engine was officially named *Thomas* by the Rev. W. Awdry himself and eventually was bought by the Peterborough Railway Society and given a new home on the Nene Valley Railway. Various Thomases have appeared at preserved lines to boost visitor numbers but in recent years all such events have been licensed by an American franchise that acquired the rights and their charges have reduced profitability. But other special events have thrived, especially the Santa specials. Then there are special events such as those commemorating the centenary of the First World War and, of course, important dates in railway history with GWR 150 and GWR 175.

All these events make great demands on both permanent staff and the volunteer helpers. Locomotives have to be prepared and carriages require just as much tender loving care as do engines. Signals have to be manned, guards have to be on duty, stewards have to be on site, tickets sold and checked – and many, many other jobs need to be carried out to ensure a successful day. But as long as there are people with a fascination for the wonderful world of steam, there will be visitors to entertain and a willing body of enthusiasts to make sure they enjoy the experience.

Chapter Eleven

Seeing Stars

Many films and TV dramas are set in the past, often at a time when the steam railway was one of the main forms of transport. And in order to recreate those days, producers have to turn to preservation societies to provide them with appropriate settings, locomotives and rolling stock. In a few cases, certain lines will forever be associated with the films made there – *The Railway Children* being the best-known example. Even today, nearly fifty years after the film first appeared, passengers on the Keighley & Worth Valley Railway still half expect to see the children running down the hill to wave at them as they pass the house that was their filmic home. Didcot is not so easily recognisable in any film, not because it hasn't had its share of film crews, but because it has mostly been disguised as somewhere else – and in the very first appearance of a Didcot locomotive in a major film, even the engine was unrecognisable. The film was *The Bliss of Mrs. Blossom* made in 1968 and starring Shirley MacLaine. The sequence was filmed at Taplow and involved locomotive 6106 decked out in startling psychedelic designs. What the old gentlemen of the GWR would have thought doesn't bear thinking about. This was not the only engine to undergo a transformation; the next in line had a far more demanding role to play.

After long negotiations, an agreement was reached to hire out locomotive 1466 for a role in Richard Attenborough's movie *Young Winston*, starring Simon Ward in the title role. The sequence was to record an incident in the Boer War that involved the capture of a British train with Churchill on board, that led to his imprisonment. As everyone knows, the Boer Wars were all fought in Africa, but this being cinema it was to be filmed in Wales. The chosen site was on the old Neath and Brecon line that at that time was still open for quarry traffic between Colbern Junction and Craig-y-Nos. This was to be a challenging route for the old engine, with steep gradients as severe as 1 in 50.

On 3 May 1971, 1466 set off for Wales accompanied by Toad 68684 that carried a variety of spares and tools that might be needed, during the locomotive's seven-week stay on location. Stan French, a British Rail Western Region locomotive inspector and GWS member, was in charge, and during his stay he would be joined by a number of GWS volunteers who had given up holiday time to help out. Some might have thought that life on a film location would be rather glamorous; they were soon to be disillusioned. The film company had supplied caravans for accommodation, handily situated close to the local pub, but they would have little enough time to spend there; the days were long and unrelenting. Stan French wrote an account of the filming for the GWS Newsletter.

The first couple of days were spent on steam chests that involved some remedial work to a leaking regulator gland. Then the engine had to be transformed from its Great Western locomotive state to an armoured South African version. The 'armour plating' was flimsy plywood painted with metallic paint to give the right effect. Large wooden sleepers were attached to the buffer beam and by the time the job was completed almost all that could be seen of the original 1466 was the chimney. After that it was down to business. As the crew were required to be on location at 7.15 in the morning, this

1466, heavily disguised as an armoured Boer War train, in an action scene from *Young Winston* being filmed in Wales.

meant leaving the base at seven. Early starts were very much the order of the day – usually at 5 a.m. when the first task was to take on water from a stand pipe in the middle of the road – any local residents getting up that early would have turned on their taps in vain. Then there was all the usual business of filling the bunker and raising steam. Once on site, it was unremittingly busy until a very welcome breakfast break at 10.30, then back again for the rest of a long day, with breaks for lunch and tea. Filming usually went on to 8 or 8.30 in the evening – then it was back again to do all those essential jobs on the engine before they could either retire wearily to their beds or get in a quick restorative pint before closing time. Then it was all to do again the next day. Even when not being actually filmed, the engine was used to transport equipment, puffing its way up the steep slope. Inevitably, there were many interesting events to record as the weeks went by.

A sequence was being shot during which the Boers were attacking the train. There had already been 23 takes and in the middle of the 24th the dome joint blew with an alarming bang that created a certain amount of panic among the extras called in as Boers, who assumed the whole thing was about to blow up. Things were rapidly brought under control; steam pressure reduced and 1466 limped back to base with only 30psi showing on the gauge by the time she finally came to a halt. Tony Matthews was sent off in his car to find suitable joining material and the gang got to work on repairing the damage. Amazingly, they had completed the task by 8 o'clock that night and half an hour later the engine had been successfully steamed and declared fit for work the next day.

Film people are not, as a general rule, very conversant with the intricacies of steam locomotives and sometimes their requests proved difficult to meet if not impossible. On one occasion, the direction came out that the engine was to speed as fast as it would go and when it reached top speed the stunt men, playing soldiers, would leap for safety. Stan French confirmed that he could certainly get up a good speed, possibly as high as 70mph, a suggestion that was met with some scepticism. 1466 rocketed down the bank with the regulator opened wide and did indeed reach 70 but very wisely the stunt men remained in their vehicles. It was agreed that a more modest speed of 25mph would be quite sufficient if any of the leaping soldiers were to survive the experience without serious injury.

Often, the drivers were required to work with extremely narrow margins. A crucial scene was the train crash, when one train had been derailed and the other was approaching at speed and was required to halt just in time with only an inch or two to spare. The rolling stock was all imitation, made of lightweight material, but even so, had 1466 slammed into them at speed there would have been an awful lot of repairs needed before they could do another take. For the sake of the drama, the engine had to be travelling at speed and brought to an emergency stop, ideally with the buffers just touching the end of the derailed train in front of it. This meant slamming on the brakes and allowing the vacuum to fall to a meagre three inches. The strewn 'rolling stock' was held in place by a manned crane. As the locomotive sped towards the wreckage, the crane crew were convinced it would never stop in time and bolted. But in the event the whole thing went off perfectly.

On another occasion, an assistant director appeared with the instructions that the driver was to approach a given spot at speed and stop by a chalk mark. There was a minor problem – no one in the cab could actually see the chalk mark. Nevertheless, its site was indicated by the film crew and Stan French did his best. After nineteen failed attempts, Stan announced to the assistant that he would be perfect next time. Not surprisingly the assistant was more than a little sceptical but, as Stan pointed out, they had better get it right as there wasn't enough coal left in the bunker for another try. To everyone's amazement, he hit within a millimetre of the infamous mark to be greeted by a typically filmic response – 'Very well done ducky'. By the end of the seven weeks, the film company had all the shots they needed and 1466 could return to Didcot for a well-earned rest, but not before the gang had celebrated the end of filming in the local. Multiple takes and long periods of waiting around are all too typical of all film work and they would occur again and again as Didcot became home to a variety of film crews.

The story of the chalk mark reminded me of another day's filming at Didcot, one in which I was personally involved, presenting a programme with Ray Gosling. The BBC made a TV documentary to celebrate GWR 150. It was slightly fraught, as the original intention had been to have a long sequence shot at Swindon works, but just before filming was to start, BR announced that the works were to close and we were not allowed in. That left something of a hole in the programme, so the director was determined to make the most of filming a live locomotive in steam at Didcot. It was decided to have a dramatic shot of the engine heading straight at the cameraman. He agreed to take up a position between the rails, staring straight

Society volunteers dressed as Russian railway workers at the beginning of the twentieth century for Peter Brook's film *Meetings with Remarkable Men* of 1979.

at the oncoming train. Again, the driver was given a chalk mark – this time he got it right first time, much to the cameraman's relief. That day I was mightily impressed by the driver's skill – and glad I wasn't a cameraman.

1466 was not the only Didcot locomotive to appear on screen at that time. *Cookham Manor*, coupled to one of the Ocean coaches, was called into service for a sketch featuring Ronnie Corbett as part of the popular TV series *The Two Ronnies*. Life was a lot simpler than it had been on location in Wales. TV directors have neither the time nor the budgets to indulge in elaborate set-ups involving multiple takes – though the latter are not unknown. Ronnie Corbett was to watch the train leave and rather than go to the expense of getting up steam and moving the train forward, it was far cheaper and simpler to put the actor on a trolley and move him backwards. On screen the effect was, of course, exactly the same.

Over the coming years, Didcot and its stock were to be involved in many film and TV dramas and documentaries. They serve a

Glenda Jackson as Sarah Bernhardt in *The Incredible Sarah.*

Sir Gerald Nabarro was a great railway enthusiast and clearly made the most of his visit to Didcot.

dual purpose; they provide very welcome publicity and bring in very useful sums of money. One other locomotive made an early film appearance – *Bonnie Prince Charlie* was in *The Heroes of Telemark* but as that happened in 1964 before the locomotive was taken into preservation it doesn't really qualify for the Didcot list of filmic honours. But it was not only locomotives that were transformed for filming; many of the Didcot buildings have also appeared in some unlikely disguises.

There are some films that are set in historic periods in which scenes have been set in specific railway stations. British Rail were never going to stop all regular services to fill their station with steam locomotives and actors in costume, so alternatives had to be found. Unlikely as it might seem, in the 2004 TV film *Carrie's War*, the site chosen to represent Paddington was the transfer shed. Needless to say, there were not many long shots. The engine shed has also had its share of makeovers. In *The Incredible Sarah,* the 1971 movie in which Glenda Jackson played Sarah Bernhardt, the building stood in for stations in both Dover and Paris, while in the TV version of *Three Men in a Boat* it stood in for Waterloo. By far the most spectacular adaptation came in 2012, when the engine shed was transformed into a Moscow station for *Anna Karenina* with Keira Knightley. The lifting shop, on the other hand, remained more or less itself when Peter Brook arrived to direct his life of the mystic G. I. Gurdjieff, *Meetings with Remarkable Men,* in 1979. It was a sequence in a busy engineering workshop, with the men hard at work on various locomotives. The only difference was that it was supposed to be in Russia not Oxfordshire and the various GWS members who took part were dressed in appropriate costumes. Apparently, they thought it was all great fun and it is doubtful if many were aware that there were many young actors who would actually have paid good money just to be able to add to their CV that they had been in a movie directed by Brook.

A number of locomotives from Didcot have made film appearances in a variety of locations in works of fiction for cinema and television. There have also been a number of documentaries made and these often carry the very obvious advantage that Didcot can appear as itself. As well as the GWR 150 programme mentioned earlier, there have been two programmes devoted to Brunel, one presented by Dan Cruickshank and the other by Jeremy Clarkson. That great enthusiast for all things steaming, Fred Dibnah, came in 2003 for his series *Age of Steam* and Michael Portillo included Didcot in his *Great Railway Journeys.* Programmes like these are excellent publicity showing what Didcot has to offer to an audience that can run into millions.

In 2018, a new museum, Being Brunel, was opened next to the engineer's iconic ship, the SS *Great Britain.* Among the visitor attractions is a film telling the story of the broad gauge, much of which was shot at Didcot using *Firefly.* Both Daniel Gooch and Brunel himself put in appearances, in the shape of actors Will Bryant and Patrick Evans. Brunel and Gooch were not the only famous visitors to Didcot over the years and they covered a wide spectrum of backgrounds and interests. An early visitor was the Member of Parliament and railway enthusiast Sir Gerald Nabarro, he of the extravagant moustache. He was clearly not intending just to be a spectator as he arrived with his boiler suit and spent a very enjoyable day. An equally exuberant personality but from a very

different world also visited later on. Timmy Mallett made his name with his series 'Timmy on the tranny' and later TV shows, but early in his career he worked just down the road at Radio Oxford. Even in those early days, he was seen as a rather zany character – the only member of staff who regularly came to the office on roller skates. He certainly brought a touch of jollity to the Railway Centre. There were, of course, many distinguished guests from the world of railways, such as Lord Faulkner and Sir Peter Porter, and all were made welcome. Their visits also helped to bring publicity, but equally importantly, they demonstrated that Didcot Railway Centre was a place to be taken seriously for its stalwart efforts to preserve the best of the Great Western Railway while at the same time offering a thoroughly pleasurable experience to all visitors of all ages and backgrounds.

Princess Anne's visit to Didcot in 2003.

CHAPTER TWELVE

Conclusion

The story of the Great Western Society has been an extraordinary one. That it was started over half a century ago by a group of schoolboys is itself remarkable enough, but what makes it all the more amazing is that railway restoration was still very much in its infancy. The very first standard gauge line based on the historic Middleton Colliery Railway had only been preserved and taken over by amateurs in 1960. There were few precedents for them to follow but somehow, they achieved their initial goal of obtaining a 14xx locomotive and a coach to go with it, even if there was really no home for either when they started out. Yet from this modest beginning a whole enterprise has developed at the Society's permanent home at Didcot that shows off the achievements of the Great Western Railway through the years through its unique collection of locomotives, rolling stock, signalling, buildings and

The Society will continue to flourish as long as it still attracts young volunteers who are happy to, literally, do the dirty work.

museum. It has become a collection of not merely national but international importance, tracing the development of the steam railway from its earliest days to the end of steam – and even a little beyond. From a Society whose initial membership could all get together in a single room, it has grown to one with literally thousands of members from all over the world.

As the enterprise grew, with visitor numbers running into the tens of thousands, it became essential to employ a few key staff on a full time basis, but the bulk of the work is still down to the enthusiasm of amateur volunteers. Some have brought specialist skills, essential when it came to the more technical aspects of restoration, which could be anything from installing a signalling system to recreating a working locomotive. But there have always been those ready and willing to take on all the unglamorous jobs that are so necessary, from laying track to pouring concrete – cleaning locomotives, not

Working at Didcot is by no means a male-only preserve. Laura Davidson spent her birthday one year training to become a guard.

driving them. And, of course, there are the many members who have contributed money and often valuable relics. Nothing on this scale could have been achieved without this enthusiastic army of helpers, each playing their part, no matter how insignificant it might seem to outsiders.

The Great Western Railway was much loved by those who travelled on it in the past and it seems its memory is equally cherished today. And as long as there are men and women, girls and boys who still believe that the letters GWR really do stand for God's Wonderful Railway, Didcot should survive and flourish for many more years to come. These sentences may mark the end of this book, but they do not signify the end of the story. One thing is absolutely certain: there will be changes made over the coming years, and given the history of the Society so far, they will make a splendid institution even greater.

Index